2/2000

2/2000

EARTH

The Making of a Planet

EARTH
The Making of a Planet

by Roy A. Gallant
and Christopher J. Schuberth

MARSHALL CAVENDISH   NEW YORK

The authors wish to thank Dr. Jerry LaSala, astrophysicist and chairman of the Department of Physics, the University of Southern Maine, for reviewing the various chapters and passages of this book dealing with astronomy.

Marshall Cavendish, 99 White Plains Road, Tarrytown, New York 10591

Library of Congress Cataloging-in-Publication Data
Gallant, Roy A.
Earth: the making of a planet / by Roy A. Gallant and Christopher J. Schuberth.
    p.   cm.
Includes bibliographical references and index.
Summary: Examines the formation, size, rocks and minerals, crust, mantle, climate, oceans, and other features of our planet.
ISBN 0-7614-5012-2
1. Earth—Juvenile literature. [1. Earth.] I. Schuberth, Christopher J. II. Title
QB631.4.G35   1998   550—dc21   97-13224   CIP   AC

The text of this book is set in 11 point Berkeley Book
Printed in the United States of America.
First edition

6   5   4   3   2   1

For Melissa, Martha, and Max—R.A.G.

To my wife, Judith, naturally,
 for her uncompromising support—
and to our students,
who, complainingly at times,
have often been our best teachers—C.J.S.

Contents

Galaxies and stars are born out of gigantic clouds of gas and space dust. These three columns form part of the Eagle Nebula located in the constellation Serpens, about 7,000 light-years from us. Our entire Solar System would be dwarfed by one of the fingerlike projections. The photograph was taken by the Hubble Space Telescope. NASA

1
Birth of the Sun and Planets

The Universe Begins

Not very long ago, at least as measured by cosmic time, there was only an immense, overpowering darkness. There was no planet Earth. Our local *star*, the Sun, did not exist. Neither did that vast city of some three hundred billion suns, the Milky Way galaxy. There were no galaxies at all and no one to record the tumultuous event that was about to happen.

Astronomers say that it was the most fantastic explosion imaginable. What was to become every piece of matter and every breath of energy in the Universe came into existence from a tiny cosmic superatom. Sometime between twelve and twenty billion years ago, that superatom exploded in what has come to be called the *Big Bang*. At that moment, time and the Universe began. The fireball explosion of the Big Bang sent energy rushing off in all directions. The Universe began to grow larger, and it has been expanding ever since, all the galaxies hurtling away from one another.

Just after the explosion, if that is what actually happened, nearly all of the Universe was a hot cloud of hydrogen. Hydrogen is the simplest of the more than one hundred known chemical *elements*. Over the next several seconds, some of the hydrogen particles joined and formed the second-simplest element, helium. Then over the next minute or so, as the young Universe kept expanding, the hydrogen spread out so thinly that no more fusions could take place. Only a few minutes after the Universe began, nine-tenths of the matter in it was hydrogen nuclei and one-tenth helium.

Galaxies and Stars Form

We now move the cosmic clock ahead about a hundred thousand to a million years. The scene we find is one of great clouds of hydrogen and helium, all rushing away from one another. Those clouds are to evolve into the countless billions of galaxies captured as images by the Hubble Space Telescope. As far as we can tell, all the *galaxies* seem to be between ten

There appears to be no end to the galaxies that can be photographed through telescopes. Galaxies of many shapes are seen in this galactic cluster visible in the constellation Hercules. MOUNT WILSON AND LOS CAMPAÑAS OBSERVATORIES, CARNEGIE INSTITUTION OF WASHINGTON

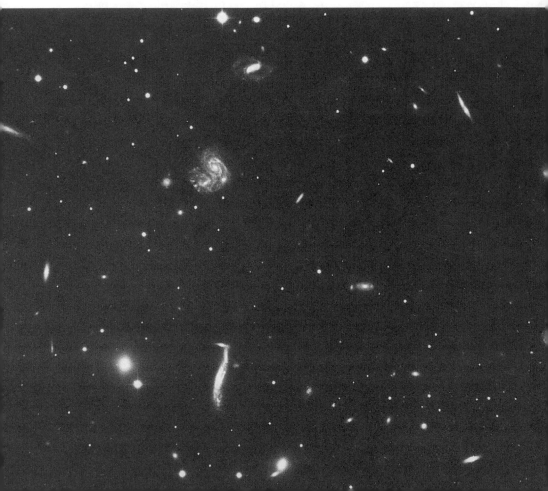

This globular cluster of stars seen in the constellation Hercules is typical of other such clusters, which are made up of hundreds of thousands to millions of stars. MOUNT WILSON AND PALOMAR OBSERVATORY

billion and fifteen billion years old. That is more than twice the age of the Sun.

We can imagine those early *proto*galaxies, or galaxies in the making, as wheeling islands of hydrogen and helium. They are separated by unimaginable distances of dark and nearly empty space. Hundreds of billions of lumpy, local clouds of hydrogen and helium begin to form within each protogalaxy. The more massive and tightly packed clouds gravitationally attract and gobble up less massive ones and grow at their expense. For millions of years chaos rules, but order is in the making. It comes as the matter of the more massive clouds begins to organize into giant spheres. Gravity is the organizer, packing and heating the spheres until they begin to glow as individual stars like the Sun and as clusters of stars.

We move our cosmic clock ahead once more. The time is now some five billion years ago, and the place is out near the edge of our home galaxy, the

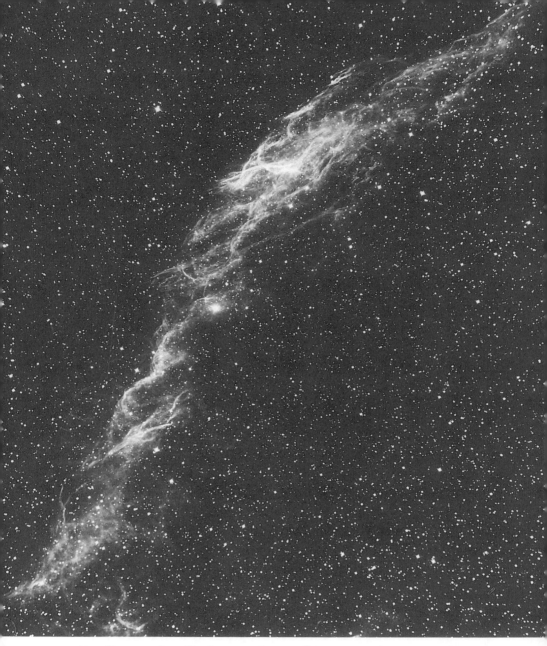

Fine filaments of gas, like this one in the constellation Cygnus the Swan, are the remains of matter cast off by exploding stars called supernovas. The clouds contain atoms of heavy elements forged by the supernova on exploding. Such a cloud of cast-off matter most likely mixed with, and so enriched, the cloud of matter out of which the Sun and planets were formed. MOUNT WILSON AND LOS CAMPAÑAS OBSERVATORIES, CARNEGIE INSTITUTION OF WASHINGTON

Milky Way. One of those giant clouds of hydrogen, helium, and cosmic dust has, over millions of years, been collecting matter, collapsing in on itself, and heating up as a protostar. It shares its cosmic neighborhood with other stars—some younger, others older, and still others so old that they are in their death throes. In the process of aging and dying, an especially massive star forges, in its hot core, elements heavier than hydrogen and helium and then explodes. Such heavy elements include carbon, oxygen, silicon, and iron. Some of the elements clump as compounds and form cosmic dust. We call these exploding stars *supernovas*.

The cloud of heavy elements cast off by one such supernova just happens to mix with the hydrogen and helium cloud of the protoSun. Enriched with those heavy elements, our solar cloud continues its process of gravitational collapse. As its matter keeps tumbling in toward the core, three things happen: When any gas is compressed, it heats up, and so the collapsing cloud grows hotter and hotter, until its glow changes from a dull red to a yellowish white light. Second, as more and more matter collects in the core region, any slight rotation the cloud had is magnified, much as a skater spins faster as she draws her outstretched arms in toward her sides. So the cloud begins to spin faster. Finally, the rapid spinning causes the outer parts to flatten out, like a pizza crust spun in the air.

For a hundred million years this drama unfolds, until finally the temperature in the Sun's core reaches some ten million degrees. The crushing pressure and intense heat combine and ignite the nuclear furnace that fuses hydrogen into helium. It is just such *fusion* reactions that keep the Sun shining as we see it shining today. In the process, the Sun changes matter into all the known forms of energy, including heat and light. In one second the Sun pours out more energy than we humans have used in all the time we have inhabited this planet. The Sun's fuel is the vast store of hydrogen in its core region. It has been converting its core hydrogen mass into energy for five billion years; and it has enough hydrogen left to shine for about another five billion years. It will then reach the end of its life span. All stars must one day go out when they can no longer convert their mass into energy. (The Sun's fate as a dying star will be described in detail in chapter 11.)

The Planets Form

Imagine that we are poised high above the new Sun some five billion years ago. We would see a central ball of fire rimmed by a broad spinning disk of gases and cosmic debris stretching away seemingly forever. The new Sun had by that time organized its matter for nuclear energy production. But the surrounding disk material was a chaos of gas, clumps of atoms forming dust grains and ices. It would take another hundred million years or so for these materials to collide and stick together as objects called *planetesimals*—rocks mixed with iron and other metals, and boulders the size of mountains. The sticking force was gravity.

As some planetesimals collided, they shattered. Others were nudged into new orbits that sent them to a fiery death in the Sun. Still others were sent on courses out of the disk as cosmic exiles. The more massive clumps gravitationally swept up less massive ones and grew larger. If they were larger than about 200 miles across, gravity pulled them into a sphere shape. If they were smaller, they remained irregular lumps, like the two moons of Mars and the asteroid Ida.

The larger sphere-shaped objects were the protoplanets. As each one acquired enough mass to withstand collisions by lesser planetesimals, it nevertheless continued to be bombarded for millions of years. We have very convincing proof of such cosmic violence in the early Solar System. The Moon has thousands of impact craters. There are more than one hundred fifty impact craters still visible on Earth. And there are thousands more on Mercury, Mars, and the moons of the gas-giant planets.

Most of the action, however, seems to have been near the Sun, where the disk matter circled faster than at Jupiter's and the other gas giants' distance. Violence reigned supreme in the region where the inner planets Mercury, Venus, Earth, and Mars were formed. Lower temperatures farther out in the disk permitted volatile materials such as methane and ammonia to solidify into planetesimals. There were more and larger planetesimals out in this region, and they built up into very large planets with cores of rock and metal.

Unlike the less massive inner planets, the more massive outer ones—

Jupiter, Saturn, Uranus, and Neptune—attracted and held onto large amounts of disk gases. Among those gases were hydrogen, helium, methane, and ammonia. Such gases make up the bulk of the outer planets' atmospheres today, but they are not present in the atmospheres of the inner, *terrestrial planets* because of the higher temperatures in those atmospheres.

The planetesimals that orbited between Mars and Jupiter had an interesting fate: Jupiter's strong gravitation prevented them from collecting into a planet. To this day they swarm as billions of pieces of rock and metal called *asteroids* and *meteoroids*. Occasionally, these rogue members of the Solar System collide and speed off along new orbits that may send them crashing into Earth. One such errant missile crashed into Earth sixty-five million years ago and probably spelled doom to dinosaurs and numerous other animals and plants. Scientists think they have found the crater formed by the asteroid in the seafloor off the coast of the Yucatán Penin-

Asteroid Ida was photographed by the Galileo space probe from a distance of 2,175 miles (3,500 kilometers). Only the second asteroid to be approached by a space probe, Ida is a giant, about 32 miles (52 kilometers) long. It is probably a stony fragment broken off by a collision with another asteroid. NASA

sula. Another such object crashed into the Arizona desert about fifty thousand years ago. Still another exploded over a desolate Siberian forest on the morning of June 30, 1908, in what is the most destructive known explosion of a cosmic body in the history of civilization.

At the outermost edge of the solar disk, there remained a spherical halo of ices that enclosed the Sun and its young family of planets in a frigid cocoon. This cloud of trillions of "dirty snowballs," as one astronomer has called them, is the Solar System's main store of comets. Whenever a passing star's gravity disturbs this cloud of comets, it flings one or more of them in toward the Sun. The famous comet named Shoemaker-Levy-9 that crashed into Jupiter in 1994 became one such cosmic missile, as did the giant comet Hale-Bopp of 1997. A second but lesser store of comets called the Kuiper Belt lies closer to us, a bit beyond Pluto. In 1997, astronomers discovered one Kuiper Belt ice ball some 300 miles (483 kilometers) across. Pluto may well be a giant Kuiper Belt object that escaped the belt and settled into an orbit about the Sun as an imposter "planet."

Long after the planets had formed, the Solar System was still a dusty and dark place. Eventually, however, streams of particles from the Sun, called the *solar wind*, swept space between the planets clean of remaining dust, but not all of it. To this day a thin veil of dust remains, and we see it as the dimly shining *zodiacal light*.

The utter chaos of the early Solar System has long been replaced by a beautifully stable—for a while, at least—Sun and system of planets

Meteor Crater, in Winslow, Arizona, was caused by an iron asteroid strike about fifty thousand years ago. The blast left a hole as deep as a six-story building and the size of fifteen football fields. UNIVERSITY OF ARIZONA

In 1908 either a comet or a stony asteroid exploded over a heavily forested region of north central Siberia and devastated an area of more than 770 square miles (2,000 square kilometers). This photograph was taken twenty-eight years after the explosion and shows the resulting wasteland, with only skeletons of trees remaining. COURTESY: COMMITTEE ON METEORITES, RUSSIAN ACADEMY OF SCIENCES

ordered by the laws of motion and gravitation. We now think that planets more often than not may be the by-products of star formation, and that we, along with planet Earth, are made up of the chemical elements of the original solar disk cloud. We, too, are by-products of star formation. Atoms that long ago were exploded out of a distant, dying star and mixed into the gas and dust of our solar cloud some five billion years ago are now part of our very bodies.

The truly remarkable thing about all of this is not that it has happened, but that, in the words of the late astronomer Carl Sagan, "a mindless selective process can convert chaos into order." We will meet that process elsewhere in this book, for given a source of energy and matter, it is the way nature works.

In that mysterious vastness that is the Universe, the Solar System occupies a minuscule patch of space at the outer edge of a galaxy called the Milky Way. And within what appears to us as the vastness of the Solar System is a small sphere of rock and metal adorned with life, bathed with water, and protected within a soft cocoon of air. It is time that we sharpen our focus and examine that cosmic jewel we call Earth.

2

Earth in Its Youth

Geological forces act all around us day and night. Molten rock from Earth's deep interior is squeezed out onto the surface through volcanoes and cracks in the seafloor, like toothpaste from a tube. The molten rock cools and hardens. Over time, frost, water, wind, and chemical change wear it down to bits and pieces of gravel, sand, and mud. Then over still more time, those materials collect, are crushed under their own weight, and are changed by heat and pressure to form new rock. That new rock then may be thrust up as mighty mountain ranges that grace our planet for a while, only to be worn down to dust once again. And so the geological processes of erosion and transformation of Earth matter have continued from the time our planet was formed out of the gas and dust of space. And it can be expected to continue for billions of years more, perhaps until the Sun dies.

An Age for Earth

With the aid of *atomic clocks*, scientists can estimate planet Earth's age. We seem to be some 4.5 billion years old. That is the best estimate we have come up with so far. The oldest Earth materials, dated with atomic clocks that tick off the decay rate of radioactive elements, are zircon crystals from Perth, Australia. Those crystals are 4.3 billion years old. But there must have been still older Earth rocks that long ago melted and resolidified over and over again. Because they conceal their origins from us, they are beyond our ability to date by any means.

In its early youth, Earth was a fiery-hot world glowing reddish in the dark chaos of the solar disk that still circled the young Sun. Each rocky or metallic missile that smashed into our youthful planet added heat to Earth and kept it as a soupy ball of molten rock and metals, at a temperature of about 3,600 degrees Fahrenheit (3,600°F), or 2,000 degrees Celsius (2,000°C). Meanwhile, *radioactive heating* from within also helped keep the planet molten. The main ingredients of the cosmic cloud out of which Earth formed were hydrogen, helium, carbon, nitrogen, oxygen, silicon, iron, nickel, aluminum, gold, uranium, sulfur, and phosphorus. There were cosmic icebergs, as well. As they were swept up by Earth, they were instantly changed to steam that shrouded the planet in a cocoon of water vapor.

An Atmosphere and Seas

During Earth's molten and early cooling stages, many gases bubbled out of solution and collected above the new planet as a primitive atmosphere. Among such gases were large amounts of hydrogen, water vapor, nitrogen, carbon monoxide, and carbon dioxide, along with smaller amounts of methane, ammonia, and hydrogen sulfide. The air also was thick with poisonous cyanide and formaldehyde. At this stage there was little or no oxygen. The water released from the crustal rock of basalt entered the air as countless geysers. But it was so hot that the fountains of water simply evaporated into water vapor, which hung in the air.

As more and more water vapor collected in the primitive atmosphere, the air eventually cooled enough for the vapor to condense and fall as rain. In some areas, where the surface rock was cool enough, the rain soaked into the dry rock. In other areas, where the rock was still very hot, the rains evaporated back into water vapor and were driven skyward by the heat of the surface. At this stage there was no life of any kind on Earth.

As the crustal rock continued to cool, torrential rains fell day and night for perhaps a hundred thousand years and collected in pools that in time formed shallow, warm seas. By about 3.9 billion years ago, a thin, solid crust of rock floated uneasily on a vast sea of molten rock that lay beneath. Sometimes this thin crust was punctured by eruptions from below, and molten rock welled up, evaporating some seas and melting huge areas of solid crust. Other times the thin crustal rock was struck and ruptured from above by orbiting mountain-size planetesimals. The planetesimals, meteoroids, and other debris from space continued to burn down through the atmosphere and plummet to Earth, exploding into vast clouds of dark dust. Fiery volcanic plumes and continual lightning brightened the night sky, as did the reddish glow of mammoth lava flows that poured out of openings in the crust.

Meanwhile, forces from the Sun were at work. Ultraviolet energy was breaking down some of the complex gases of Earth's air. It changed ammonia into free hydrogen and nitrogen; methane into carbon and hydrogen; and water vapor into hydrogen and oxygen. The free hydrogen was so light that most of it escaped Earth's gravitational grip. Many such reactions must have taken place in the chemical factory of that early atmosphere.

If Earth scientists are correct, some four hundred million years after our planet had developed a cool and generally stable rock crust, it accumulated shallow seas and had a new atmosphere containing carbon dioxide, carbon monoxide, water vapor, nitrogen, neon, and argon. Gone were the ammonia and methane of former times; still to come was the age of oxygen. And come it did, possibly beginning some two billion years ago. It came with the rise of certain oxygen-producing organisms called *cyanobacteria*. Possibly by six hundred million years ago, the air contained about the same amount of oxygen that it does today, some 21 percent. The remaining 79 percent is mostly nitrogen, with 1 percent of argon and traces of several other gases.

As the molten rock and metal materials churned within Earth, the heaviest matter, such as iron and nickel, sank into the core region. At the same time, lighter materials floated to the surface. Such materials were mostly lightweight silicate rock. This stage of Earth's formation is appropriately called the Hadean (meaning "hell-like") stage.

Slowly, Earth's surface began to cool and solidify, although gases bubbled up through eruptions of *magma*, or molten rock. Among the gases that were providing Earth with an atmosphere was water vapor. As this gas rose into the atmosphere, it cooled and condensed as rain. The water flowed as streams and rivers into the young planet's thousands of impact craters and great basins, thereby forming the first ponds and seas.

A discovery made in the mid-1980s suggests that part of Earth's vast water supply could have come from space in the form of small comets about the size of a house. Researchers in 1997 said they have spotted evidence of such comet ice balls, some forty thousand a day, raining down on Earth at the rate of five to thirty a minute. Each contains about 40 tons of water. We never see the comets because they are torn apart at distances hundreds to thousands of miles away from Earth and changed into clouds of water vapor. The clouds are then drawn into the atmosphere and eventually condense and fall as rain. Atmospheric scientists estimate that this process of comet rain has been going on for hundreds of millions of years, adding an inch or so (2.5 centimeters) of water every twenty thousand years. Over Earth's long history, that could add up to an ocean or two. Interestingly, the comet water also contains a rich array of carbon compounds, molecules of a kind that could have nurtured the origin of life on our planet.

About four billion years ago, Earth acquired its continents of the lightweight crustal rock granite, while the ocean floors acquired their heavyweight crustal rock of basalt. But the continents have never been the stable, seemingly immovable landmasses that are suggested by a classroom globe. The continents journey about as homeless migrants carried on enormous plates of mostly basalt. *Continental drift* and *plate tectonics* are the terms geologists use to describe Earth's crustal restlessness, which we will examine more closely in a later chapter. In recent years, scientists have shown that many undersea mountain ridges form a continuous global chain some 43,000 miles (69,000 kilometers) long. Hundreds of miles wide in some places, the chain snakes its way around the globe and sometimes pokes mountain peaks above sea level. Such peaks in the North Atlantic include Iceland, and in the South Atlantic,

Cristan da Cunha. The Red Sea and the Jordan Valley, which passes through Israel, Syria, Jordan, and Lebanon, are part of this same mountain ridge. So, too, is the Rift Valley of Ethiopia, Kenya, and Tanzania of East Africa.

Along the ridge top of the mountain chain is a rift valley. From time to time, molten rock from deep within the planet wells up through breaks in the crust, cools, and forms new surface rock. As it does, it spreads the seafloor outward on both sides of the ridge. Spreading of the seafloor in the Atlantic basin goes on at the rate of a little less than an inch (about 2 centimeters) a year. In a hundred years New York and Lisbon, Portugal, will be 8.2 feet (2.5 meters) farther apart than they are now. We can regard the continents as pale and lightweight rafts of granitic rock and the oceans' floors as being made of dark and heavier basaltic rock. Both continents and oceans are supported by a puttylike layer of still heavier rock hundreds of miles thick .

Earth Gets a Moon

Like Earth itself, our planet's one natural satellite seems to have been born out of violence. During Earth's early youth, possibly some 4.5 billion years ago, an especially large planetesimal a bit smaller than Mars may have collided with the young planet and splashed a large amount of matter into surrounding space. Some astronomers think that such an event formed the Moon. Computer models show that the splashed-off matter would have been mostly rock from Earth's crust and mantle regions along with metals from the planetesimal. Within 10 hours, most of the splashed-off debris formed into a sphere some 1,200 miles (1,931 kilometers) across.

At first, the Moon revolved around Earth much more rapidly than it does now, each revolution raising tides of molten rock on Earth. The gravitational interplay between the two bodies gradually sent the Moon on a slow outward spiral away from Earth, an event that continues to this day through the drag of Earth's ocean tides, which are raised by the Moon. Eventually, as this process continues over the next millions of years, Earth and the Moon will become gravitationally locked. The Moon will appear to hang motionless above Earth, with the same face of Earth always pointing toward the Moon. At that stage the Moon's outward spiral will have stopped.

Major Landform Changes through Time

What the continents and the rocky plates that ferry them about looked like for the first four billion years of Earth's geological history probably will never be known. But they were certainly nothing like the continents we live on today. Our best guesses about landform distribution don't begin until about 270 million years ago, during the geologic period called the Permian. Geologists tell us that the Northern Hemisphere at that time was mostly ocean, and there was a single enormous landmass called *Pangaea*, which means "All Earth." Pangaea existed from about 250 million to 150 million years ago. At that time a violent surge of hot magma from Earth's deep interior broke Pangaea apart into two lesser, but still enormous, landmasses. One is called *Gondwana*, meaning "land of the Gonds," a people who lived in present-day India. Gondwana later broke apart into smaller landmasses that came to include Africa, South America, India, Australia, and Antarctica. The other, called *Laurasia*, included what was later to become Eurasia, North America, Greenland, and Scotland.

We can get a bird's-eye view of some of the major global geological events by turning back the clock to that geological period called the Cambrian, which began about 570 million years ago. As we move from one period to the next, remember that the places we today call Europe, Siberia, the United States, and the Middle East had not yet gained the geographical identities they have today. They were squashed together and had no separate boundaries.

Cambrian: During the early Cambrian period, shallow seas covered the margins of the landmasses. Later in the period the seas spread inland. All the while, sand, clay, and other sediments were being washed into those seas and sometimes filling extremely long, shallow underwater depressions

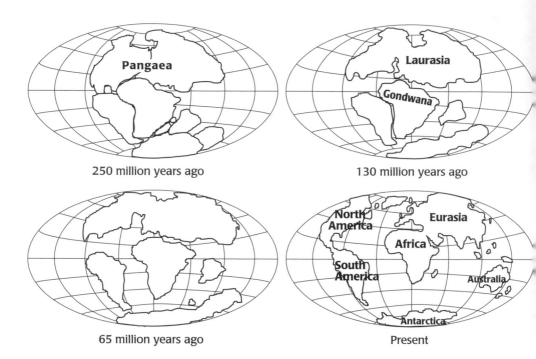

Pangaea

250 million years ago

Laurasia

Gondwana

130 million years ago

65 million years ago

North America

Eurasia

Africa

South America

Australia

Antarctica

Present

Some 250 million years ago an enormous supercontinent called Pangaea made up Earth's surface. Over time, Pangaea was broken apart by the movement of rigid "rafts" of solid rock afloat on a sea of puttylike rock. The present continents continue to move about, pushed this way and that by forces deep within the planet.

called *geosynclines*. Millions of years later, the materials in one such depression were to be thrust up as the Appalachian Mountains. More recently the Rocky Mountains were thrust up out of another and younger geosyncline.

Ordovician: The next geologic period, the Ordovician, began 500 million years ago. About 70 percent of what we now know as the Northern Hemisphere was flooded. Late in the period, crustal rock from what is now Newfoundland to the Carolinas of the United States was affected by rock transformations that led to mountain building.

Silurian: The following Silurian period, which began 440 million years ago, was a time of much volcanic activity in what today is northeastern North America. Land disturbances elsewhere produced the 3,977-mile-

(6,400-kilometer) long mountain range that today extends from Wales through Scandinavia and westward to northern Greenland. Most of that present-day land area was under water during the Silurian. Extensive salt deposits, such as those of western New York and Michigan, were formed.

Devonian: During the Devonian period, which began 400 million years ago, a land disturbance raised high mountains in New England, Quebec, and Nova Scotia. Another disturbance raised mountains along the east coast of Australia. Most of North America continued to be covered by shallow seas during most of the Devonian.

Carboniferous: The Carboniferous period began 360 million years ago and saw the sinking of widespread land areas. The result was vast lakes, swamps, and brackish lagoons where masses of vegetation were packed and transformed into coal. About half of the world's workable coal was formed during this period. Extensive mountains were raised in western Europe at this time, as were the Ouachita Mountains of Oklahoma and Arkansas. In the Southern Hemisphere there was widespread glaciation. Geologists in North America divide the Carboniferous into an older, Mississippian period and a younger, Pennsylvanian period.

Permian: It was during the Permian period, which began 290 million years ago, that Pangaea was formed. What today are Texas, Florida, and England were sitting on the Equator in Permian times. What would later become Siberia was several large islands. Many ice ages came and went, causing corresponding rises and falls in sea level. What are now the Appalachian Mountains south of New England were thrust up, and the Ural Mountains of Russia were formed. The west coast of North America saw widespread volcanic activity that altered the atmosphere by belching huge amounts of sulfuric acid into the air. Much of the western United States remained covered by shallow seas. In other parts of North America, seas were drying up and leaving vast deposits of salt and potash.

Triassic: The Triassic period began 245 million years ago. Seaways continued to cover the western edges of what are now North and South America and some parts of Europe and Asia. Extensive upwelling of dense rock occurred in the New York–New Jersey area and in South America, southern Africa, Australia, and Antarctica.

Jurassic: The Jurassic period followed the Triassic and began 205 million years ago. Jurassic seas changed little and continued to cover the western borders of North and South America. Geologically, this was a period of relative quiet, although the mountains we call the Sierra Nevada were formed. Geosyncline sinking took place along the western edges of both North and South America. In a way, the Jurassic was a stage-setting period for the great activity during the next period, the Cretaceous. Gondwana and Laurasia came into existence during this period.

Cretaceous: The Cretaceous period began 145 million years ago. Seas covered most of what is today Europe, much of Asia, and nearly half of North America. The Gulf of Mexico received nearly 11,000 feet (3,350 meters) of sediments, and it was during this period that the old geosynclines of the Cambrian were thrust up as the Rocky Mountains of North America and the Andes of South America. Midway through the Cretaceous, what are now South America and Africa began to break apart and were separated from each other by a narrow crack that grew wider at the rate of almost an inch (about two centimeters) a year. By that time, North and South America were separate continents and not linked by the land bridge of the Isthmus of Panama. India was a large island cruising northward on a collision course with Asia. When they later crunched together, the majestic peaks of the Himalayan Mountains were thrust up.

Tertiary: The Tertiary period, which began 66 million years ago, saw widespread volcanic activity in what today is the western United States. Mounts Shasta and Rainier were formed, as was the great Alpine-Himalayan mountain chain. There also was volcanic activity in the North Atlantic region, in East Africa, and in the Mediterranean region. Most of the inland seas drained and evaporated from the continents, and by the end of this period the continents had the same general outlines that they have today. Had you been able to view them from the space shuttle at that time, you would have recognized the planet as our home planet Earth.

Quaternary: The most recent geological period is the Quaternary, which began 2 million years ago. It is our period. Geologic activity called the Cascadian Disturbance deformed the Coast Ranges of the west coast of

North America and caused widespread volcanic activity. This disturbance probably is still going on today. Continental glaciers developed in North America, northern Europe, and Antarctica while valley glaciers formed in the high mountain regions. There were four named glacial and three named interglacial ages; recent evidence, however, points to many more episodes of ice. The heights of the seas varied with the formation and melting of ice.

Throughout all of the geological periods, the ceaseless twisting, churning, flooding, and drying of the land, the spewing of ash, dust, and gases into the atmosphere by volcanic activity, and the repeated grinding of massive ice flows of glacial periods shaped and reshaped the land and seas and altered global climate again and again. Those geological forces also directed the countless avenues of success and dead-end alleys of the evolution of plants and animals. They continue to do so today, and will continue to until the Sun dies.

3

Rocks and Time

We walk on an eggshell-thin layer of rock that we call Earth's crust. On average, the crust is only about 20 miles (32 kilometers) deep beneath the continents, and about half that deep beneath the oceans. The distance to Earth's center is four hundred times the thickness of Earth's crust. To our senses, all of the crustal topographic features—mountains, valleys, rivers, deep trenches in the sea—seem permanent features that have always been where we find them. But they are not. Throughout geologic time they have been formed and eroded away, and new features have replaced them. What was once land is now sea, and what have been oceans are now lands thrust up 2,000 feet (610 meters) above sea level.

To understand how Earth's topographical features are formed and reformed in an endless cycle of change, we begin with the crust itself—its minerals and rocks.

Minerals

What do these objects have in common: gold, diamonds, Styrofoam, motor oil, gasoline, the "whiteness" of paint, and the little *M* on M&M candies?

Some are minerals, which we dig directly out of the ground, such as gold and diamonds. The others are mineral products or substances that contain a certain amount of one mineral or another or come from minerals. When geologists say this or that substance is a *mineral*, they have three specific things in mind: 1) The substance is found in nature and is formed in some way by planet Earth, like gold and diamonds; 2) it has the same chemical makeup throughout, no matter where the mineral is found, again like gold and diamonds; and 3) minerals have certain *crystal* patterns that differ from one mineral to the next, but the crystal structure for each specific mineral is always the same.

A mineral also has certain physical characteristics such as color and hardness and the way it breaks. Gold, for example, is yellow and so soft that you can almost scratch it with your fingernail. Diamond is usually colorless, clear, and transparent. It is the hardest of all minerals. Nothing known in nature can scratch a diamond. Let's look at gold and diamond in a bit more detail.

Both are special kinds of minerals. What makes them special is that each is a single chemical element. While gold is gold, diamond is made up of the single element carbon. (In addition to forming diamond, carbon also naturally occurs as graphite, or the "lead" in a pencil.) Only a dozen or so out of about three thousand known minerals are made up of only a single element. All other minerals are combinations of as many as twelve or more elements. An element is any substance that cannot be broken down into a simpler substance by chemical means. Both gold and carbon are elements. Most elements can be combined with other elements to form what chemists call compounds. For example, water is a compound that is made up of the two elements hydrogen and oxygen. Again, almost all of the three thousand minerals are naturally occurring compounds.

Although some 110 elements are known, only 88 occur naturally. All the others are forged in the laboratory. Gold and carbon happen to be two that not only occur naturally but that also are not combined with other elements, although carbon can be combined with other elements through biological reactions, for instance. Elements that are found uncombined in nature are called native elements. Other examples of minerals that are native elements include sulfur, copper, platinum, and silver. Although hydrogen and oxygen are elements, they are not native elements because their atoms are not locked in place in a crystalline structure. Instead, the atoms of these two elements move about freely.

Possibly you have heard of some of the many kinds of minerals: quartz, feldspar, kaolin, mica, pyrite, galena, magnetite, and hornblende. Some of these minerals are better known than others. Quartz is perhaps the best known, since we see it the world over in beach sand or desert sand. Quartz also is needed to make all the different kinds of glass. Pyrite, which glitters like gold, is also known as fool's gold. Feldspar, mica, hornblende, magnetite, and galena are less well known. All of those minerals are forged in the great heat-and-pressure machine of Earth's interior. Kaolin, on the other hand, is formed at Earth's surface by the chemical change of feldspar when feldspar is exposed to water and carbon dioxide in the air.

Most minerals do not have any commercial value and are not of any particular use to anyone. But others are very valuable and useful. The very useful metal lead comes from galena. It is used in storage batteries, in solder, and as a shield against X rays. Kaolin is used to coat paper to make it smooth and shiny. Magnetite provides us with iron and gave ancient mariners their first magnetic compasses. Mica is used in electrical appliances. It was once used in toasters and as electrical fuses because of its resistance to electrical currents. Feldspar is an abrasive agent used in cleansing powders. Hornblende is one of those minerals that has no commercial value, so not many people have ever heard about it.

In addition to being valuable and useful, some minerals are objects of

The gemstone tourmaline occurs here attached to a quartz crystal. A gemstone is usually a mineral with especially attractive optical properties. Tourmaline comes in many colors— red, pink, blue, green, yellow, and violet, for instance. ROY A. GALLANT

Quartz crystals have well-developed, six-sided surfaces with pyramid-shaped ends. The orderly internal arrangement of a crystal's atoms gives a crystal its characteristic shape.
ROY A. GALLANT

great beauty and are regarded as the mineral equivalent of flowers of the plant world or butterflies of the animal world. Deep purple amethyst (a form of quartz) has long been a favorite the world over. Kings and queens of old wore amethyst gemstones in their crowns and royal jewelry. There is the hypnotic green of emerald, the gemstone of the mineral beryl; the wine red of garnet; or the dazzling red of ruby. And the transparent blue of sapphire, which is a gemstone of the mineral corundum; the green of malachite; the opaque blue of azurite; the shiny bronze of copper. All are favorite minerals and all are made in the pressure cookers of Earth's mysterious interior.

Minerals and Their Crystalline Structure

Ever since the invention of microscopes, the crystal structure of minerals has interested chemists and geologists. One of the most common crystals of all is ice. The ancient Greeks were fascinated by ice crystals.

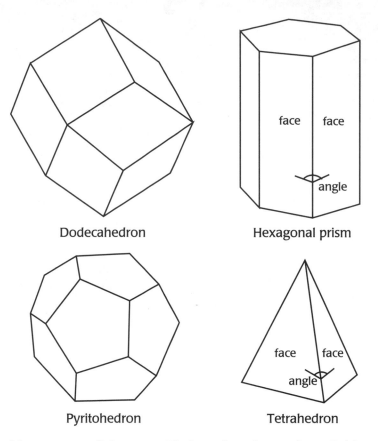

Dodecahedron   Hexagonal prism

Pyritohedron   Tetrahedron

Crystal form is a mineral's fingerprint. The flat surfaces of a crystal are called faces. The angle between them is always the same for a given crystal, regardless of its shape or size. Of the thirty-two crystal classes, four are shown here.

When they saw these glistening needles decorating the ground on a frosty morning, they marveled over the six-sided crystal structure. Despite their knowledge of mathematics and geometry, they could not understand how three-dimensional solids made from water could instantly materialize, as if by magic. They greatly admired the crystals for their beauty as objects of near perfection. They called ice *krystallos*. The Romans called it *crystallum*.

Eventually, geologists found that crystal shapes could be used to classify minerals, because each mineral displays its own individual crystal form that is not matched by any other mineral. An important discovery came in 1669 when a Danish physician, Nicolaus Steno, realized that the size of a smooth and shiny crystal face is of little importance in classifying a mineral. Instead, he learned that a mineral could be classified by the angle between two joining faces of its crystal: It was always the same for a particular crystal type regardless of the shape or size of the crystal itself. Steno suspected that the sameness of the angle of joining faces must be due to some kind of internal order of crystal particles, which were too small to see. It wasn't until 1912, when the German scientist Max von Laue examined crystals with X rays, that crystals were found to be made up of atoms packed in fixed geometric patterns, called *crystalline structure*.

You can think of crystalline structure as the way a mineral breaks apart, or *cleaves*. Some minerals cleave along planes of weakness due to weak bonding forces between the atoms and break into smooth-surfaced pieces. Mica, for example, cleaves into flat sheets about as thin as a fingernail. Quartz, on the other hand, fractures the way an ice cube does when you tap it with a spoon. Quartz fractures rather than cleaves because its atomic bonding is strong in all directions.

Another clue to crystalline structure is whether a mineral is hard or soft. Hard minerals, such as quartz and diamond, are difficult to scratch,

The crystalline structure of mica allows the mineral to split apart, or cleave, into sheets about as thin as the skin of an apple. ROY A. GALLANT

because their crystalline structures are strongly bonded. Few common minerals can scratch quartz, and no other known mineral will scratch diamond. The weak bonding of kaolin and graphite, however, allows an object as soft as the skin of your finger to scratch them and leave behind a white powder trail of kaolin or a black powder trail of graphite.

Rocks

Rocks are made of various minerals mixed and packed together. For example, the rock we know as granite usually is made up of large amounts of quartz, feldspar, and mica and small amounts of hornblende. The way the mineral mixing and packing takes place when the rock is formed determines the kind of rock. Even bits of once-living materials can make up rock or be part of it. Coal, for instance, is rock made up of old plant matter, including twigs, branches, and leaves. These former plant materials were changed by pressure and heat when the coal was formed. Fossil remains of prehistoric animals, such as dinosaur bones or seashells, are often found in other kinds of rock.

There are three major rock types, each distinguished by the way it was formed. One is called *igneous* rock, from *ignis*, the Latin word for fire. The rocks are appropriately named because they are born out of the fiery molten rock, or magma, deep under Earth's surface. When magma pours out of active volcanoes and cools on the surface, it is called lava. Examples of igneous rocks include granite, basalt, gabbro, rhyolite, diorite, and andesite.

Another type of rock is called *sedimentary* rock. Sand, gravel, mud, and silt are carried by all rivers of the world to the sea. Sometimes they release some of these sediment particles along their flood plains. Other times they deposit the sediments onto lake bottoms. Most of the sediments end up on the ocean floors. Over vast stretches of time, the loose sediments pile up and become compacted by the weight of more sediments above, and their particles are cemented together by certain chemicals in the seawater. Once consolidated, the sediments are rock. Sand hardens to form the rock called sandstone. Mud and silt are turned into shale. Pebbles form the

Samples of the three major rock types: basalt, an igneous rock (top); foliated and deformed metamorphic rock (center); sandstone, a fine-grained sedimentary rock (bottom). ROY A. GALLANT

THE ROCK CYCLE

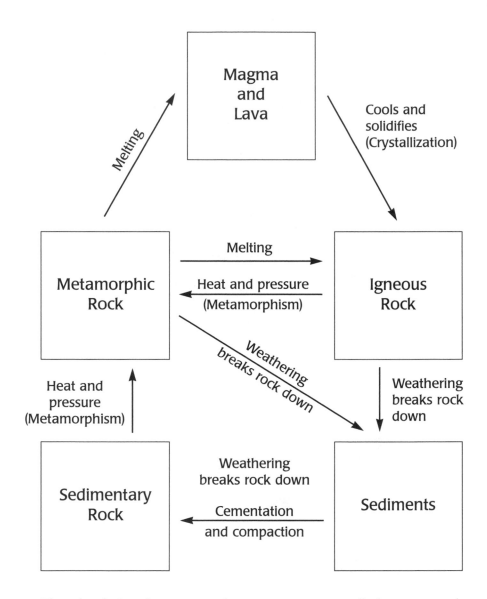

The rock cycle shows how various geologic processes are continually changing one rock type into another. While igneous and metamorphic rock are worn down into sediments that become sedimentary rock, the sedimentary rock can be changed into metamorphic rock by heat and pressure. Metamorphic rock, in turn, can be melted into igneous rock.

rock called conglomerate. Calcite, also called lime, forms in seawater and settles onto the seafloor. When it hardens, the resulting rock is called limestone. Layers of calcium carbonate skeletons of microscopic sea organisms, which rain down onto the seafloor by the billions, also harden to become limestone.

The third major rock type is called *metamorphic* rock. It has a complex origin and history. Metamorphic rock is rock that has undergone physical and chemical change. The word "metamorphic" means just that, "changed in form." High temperature and pressure deep within Earth's crust are the agents that change a rock type into metamorphic rock. Much of New England and eastern Canada are made up of metamorphic rock that was formed deep underground but after millions of years of erosion has been exposed. Examples of metamorphic rock include slate, marble, quartzite, gneiss, and schist.

The history of Earth's rocks is an endless story of change. The Sierra Nevada mountains of California are made up of the igneous rock granite. So is Stone Mountain, in Georgia. As those mountains are eroded away by rain and ice, rivers carry the sediment particles to the oceans. There the sediments accumulate and eventually are turned into sedimentary rock. Tens of millions of years later, this sedimentary rock, now deeply buried, can be transformed by heat and pressure into metamorphic rock. Likewise, igneous rock can be remelted and become igneous rock of a new generation.

That grand recycling scheme is called the *rock cycle*, and it tells us there is no beginning and no end to a rock's physical evolution. No new material is created, and no existing material is destroyed. All Earth materials are cycled among the three igneous, sedimentary, and metamorphic environments.

Sedimentary Rocks and the History of Life

It is the sedimentary rocks that are of special interest to us when we want to find out about past life on planet Earth. Equally interesting is the way the secrets of sedimentary rocks were revealed. In the early 1800s, the English land surveyor William Smith was laying out plans for the construction of canals in the south of England. During his digging to learn about the kinds of rocks he would have to deal with, he discovered that they were of sedimentary types arranged "like slices of bread and butter," he said.

As he studied the pattern of the layers, or strata, he soon learned to identify each one. He became especially interested in the appearance of plant and animal fossils in each layer. After a while, Smith was able to identify the individual layers of any sedimentary rock sample collected anywhere in southern England. From the kinds of fossils each layer contained, he was also able to read the time sequence in which the strata were laid down.

What Smith discovered is that plant and animal types change over time. Old populations of plants and animals found in older and deeply buried layers no longer appeared in younger and shallower sedimentary rock layers. The older populations appeared to become extinct with time and other, new populations to take their places. No two different layers of sedimentary rock seemed to contain the same kinds of fossils. Smith became so skilled at identifying fossils that he preferred not to look at the actual rock anymore, just the fossils. Using only the fossils, Smith could tell quickly what specific layer of sedimentary rock his workers were digging through.

Smith did not realize just how important a discovery he had made. His chief concern was building better canals, and his success depended on the rock he had to dig through. Little did he know that the neatly sequenced fossils in his samples were a key to reading rock strata over hundreds and thousands of miles across the land and oceans. Arranging sedimentary rocks by their relative age—an older layer usually lying below a younger one—led to the idea of the *geologic column*. The geologic column is an idea rather than an actual pile of rocks neatly arranged according to age over the millions of years of geologic history. If there were such an actual geologic column, it would be almost 100 miles (161 kilometers) high.

We divide this imaginary column of sedimentary rock into geologic time units called eons, eras, periods, and epochs. The strange-sounding names for the periods relate to the locations where these early sedimentary-rock

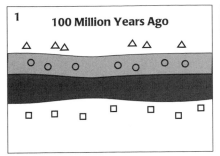

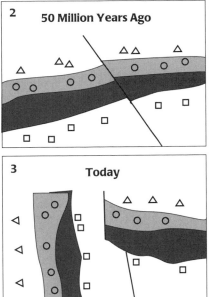

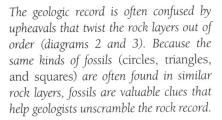

The geologic record is often confused by upheavals that twist the rock layers out of order (diagrams 2 and 3). Because the same kinds of fossils (circles, triangles, and squares) are often found in similar rock layers, fossils are valuable clues that help geologists unscramble the rock record.

studies were first carried out: Cambria was the Roman name for Wales; the Ordovices and Silures were two ancient Celtic tribes of Wales; Permian is from the Province of Perm in central Russia. Paleocene comes from the Greek for "early dawn," or "ancient time"; Pleistocene from "most recent"; Holocene from "totally recent."

Although the fossil record provided a way of telling that one rock layer was older or younger than another, it did not tell geologists the numerical age of a layer. That didn't become possible until the discovery of radioactivity in 1896. The atoms of radioactive elements such as uranium decay or change into atoms of a different element. They do this on their own because the atoms are very large and so unstable. By measuring the rate of decay of uranium into lead, for example, we can tell the age of this or that rock. We can now say that the Paleozoic (from the Greek *palaios*, meaning "ancient," and *zoe*, meaning "life") era began some 580 million years ago. The Mesozoic (from the Greek *mesos*, meaning "middle") era, the time when the dinosaurs ruled, began some 245 million years ago and ended about 66 million years ago. Finally, the Cenozoic (from the Greek *kainos*, meaning "recent") era is the era in which we live.

Importance of Minerals and Rocks

One important way scientists have come to learn about our planet is by studying its minerals, rocks, and the fossils entombed in sedimentary rock. Prehistoric peoples thousands of years ago learned how to free useful metals, such as copper and iron, from the minerals that hold these metals. In doing so, they made tools, decorative objects, and other items of value for everyday living. Today we extract and fashion thousands of products from minerals. Crude oil, for instance, comes from sedimentary rock in various parts of the world. This natural petroleum is then converted into motor oil, gasoline, kerosene, synthetic fibers, Styrofoam, and plastics. The whiteness of paint and the tiny *M* on M&M candies come from the two little-known minerals ilmenite and rutile.

Planet Earth, then, is a huge chemical laboratory, and its minerals are the results of complex interactions taking place in the crustal rock and in deep regions beneath the ocean floor.

4

Inside the Planet

What would it be like if we could dig a tunnel straight down into Earth's center and then keep going until the hole came out on the opposite side? Geologists have long imagined just such a mission. That impossible drill hole would give us direct evidence of the kinds of rock and other materials at ever deeper levels within Earth. It would also show how those materials are arranged. Since we can't drill such a hole, we must rely on other ways of finding out what the inside of the planet is like.

To begin with, such a tunnel would be 7,914 miles (12,736 kilometers) long. Since it would pass through Earth's center, it would be a measure of the planet's *diameter*. Had we stopped at the very center instead of going all the way through to the opposite side, the distance would be about 3,957 miles (6,368 kilometers), or a measure of the planet's *radius*. That's a little more than the distance from New York City to Los Angeles, California, but straight down.

Suppose you made that "radius" journey from New York to California, and then continued on across the Pacific Ocean to Tokyo, Japan, then on to New Delhi in India, Athens in Greece, Madrid in Spain, and then back across the Atlantic Ocean to New York City again. You would have journeyed about 25,000 miles (40,233 kilometers). That distance around the planet is Earth's *circumference*. You may be wondering how such measurements for Earth were first made, since no one has ever strung a tape measure around the planet or dug a tunnel through it.

Earth's circumference was first worked out more than two thousand years ago, in 235 B.C., by Eratosthenes, a Greek astronomer, geographer, and mathematician. Today, artificial satellites in orbit about the planet give us exact measurements of Earth's dimensions.

Earth's Crust and Mantle

How do we know what lies beneath Earth's thin shell of crustal rock? The deepest mines go down only about 2.5 miles (4 kilometers). The world's deepest well is in a remote northern outpost of Russia, and it is a little less than 8 miles (13 kilometers) deep. Even volcanic eruptions bring

Geologists who study Earth's interior visualize zones of various physical makeup. At the surface is the thin crustal rock, then the mantle of denser rock, and finally an outer liquid core and a solid inner core. Both cores are made of iron and nickel.

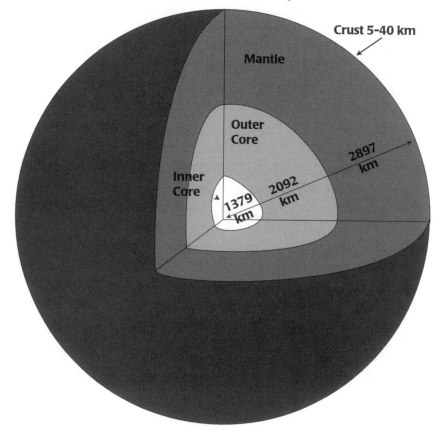

By Eratosthenes' time, scholars knew that Earth was round. That knowledge was important for the calculation of Earth's circumference that Eratosthenes was about to make. A hundred fifty years earlier, the great Aristotle had shown that Earth was a sphere: Why would a ship's mast appear lower and lower as the ship sailed over the horizon? That would not happen on a flat sea. Also, he pointed out that during a total eclipse of the Moon, the shadow that Earth casts on the Moon is curved—further proof that Earth is a sphere.

Simple observation made in the Egyptian town of Syene (today called Aswan) had told Erathosthenes that on the first day of summer, at high noon the Sun was directly overhead and shone straight down. Observation also told him that a stone post did not cast a shadow at that precise moment. But at that same moment in the city of Alexandria, some 500 miles (805 kilometers) north of Syene, the Sun was not directly overhead. Because it was not, a stone post in Alexandria *did* cast a shadow. The reason, he knew, was Earth's curved surface, as shown in the diagram.

What, you might ask, do these observations in two cities have to do with working out Earth's circumference?

Eratosthenes carefully measured the angle of the shadow of the stone post at Alexandria. It was almost exactly 7 degrees. Since 7 degrees are 1/50 of a circle, Eratosthenes reasoned that the 500-mile (805-kilometer) distance between Alexandria and Syene must be 1/50 the circumference of circular Earth. So, the circumference of Earth must be fifty times the distance between these two cities, or 25,000 miles (40,233 kilometers). He came within ½ percent of the currently accepted value of 24,860 miles (40,007 kilometers). Once Eratosthenes knew Earth's circumference, it was easy to calculate its diameter and radius.

Even more remarkable than the accuracy of Eratosthenes' measurement was the fact that Earth was so large! Many people found it hard to believe. When Columbus set out on his epic voyage in 1492 across the Atlantic Ocean, he believed that the planet was about 25 percent smaller. He thought his voyage to China would be only some 5,000 miles (8,047 kilometers). Had he realized that an additional 8,000 miles (12,874 kilometers) of sailing lay ahead of him, he probably would never have left Spain.

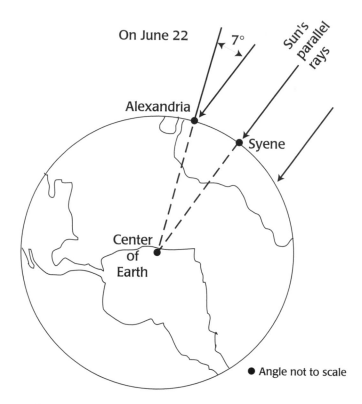

On June 22   7°   Sun's parallel rays

Alexandria

Syene

Center
of
Earth

● Angle not to scale

In 235 B.C., the Greek scholar Eratosthenes determined Earth's circumference with remarkable accuracy by using simple geometry (see text for explanation). Many scholars of the time found it hard to believe that Earth was so large.

material to the surface from a depth of only about 100 miles (161 kilometers)—a small fraction of the distance to Earth's center. What we know about Earth's interior does not come from any of the deep wells or mines. It comes, surprisingly, from seismic waves, which are waves generated by earthquakes.

An earthquake occurs somewhere on the planet about once every thirty seconds. That means there are about a million earthquakes a year. Fortunately, most are not particularly powerful. Also, most occur in unpopulated places such as the ocean floor or in remote geographic regions. Every time an earthquake rattles the planet, we have an opportunity to gather valuable information about Earth's interior.

Several types of shock waves occur during an earthquake. Those that travel along the surface are called *surface waves*; they aren't very useful in telling us about the planet's interior. However, a second group of waves, called *body waves*, is useful because they travel right through the planet. The body waves give us detailed information because their behavior changes as they pass through different materials at ever greater depths toward the remote interior.

There are two types of body waves. One is called a *P-wave*, or *primary wave*. The waves are called "primary" because they travel the fastest and so reach an earthquake station first. A P-wave moves through rock by the wave's push-and-pull effect, by an alternating compressing and expanding of the rock. P-waves are something like a slinky toy that gets squeezed and pulled apart.

The second kind of body wave is called the *S-wave*, or *secondary wave*, because it reaches the earthquake station second. S-waves vibrate the ground like a violin string, up and down and side to side. During an earthquake, both P- and S-waves leave the earthquake focus region at the same time. The focus is the actual point underground where the earthquake snaps the rock. But because the S-waves travel only two-thirds the speed of the P-waves, the P-waves are felt first. For example, a P-wave travels 100 miles (161 kilometers) twenty seconds faster than the S-wave; it travels 2,000 miles (3,219 kilometers) two minutes and fifty-four seconds faster than the S-wave. When the P- and S-waves reach Earth's surface, they trigger the surface waves, which are the ones that cause damage during an earthquake.

Scientists have learned something else about how body waves travel. For example, P-waves can travel through solids, liquids, or gases. The reason is that the particles making up all three can be compressed. But the S-waves can travel through only those materials that have a definite shape—meaning only solids. The molecules of liquids and gases slip around one another too easily, so they cannot transmit the S-waves. Scientists also learned that both types of body waves travel faster through dense or heavyweight rock such as basalt than they do through less dense or lightweight rock such as sandstone. Those two important discoveries about how P- and

S-waves travel were to play important roles in prying secrets out of the planet's interior.

In 1909, the Croatian scientist Andrija Mohorovičić was studying the wave patterns produced by P- and S-waves from recent earthquakes. The patterns suggested that Earth's inside was layered. Instead of being uniform throughout, like a bowling ball, the planet seemed to resemble an egg with its different layers: the thin outside shell, the colorless and clear liquid beneath, and the yellow yolk at the center.

Mohorovičić found that at a depth of some 20 miles (32 kilometers), the speed of the P- and S-waves suddenly increased and kept increasing. That meant the density of the rock at depths greater than 20 miles (32 kilometers) was increasing. It also meant that there must be a boundary at that 20-mile (32-kilometer) depth, one that marked a division between Earth's lightweight crustal rock and the rock beneath. That boundary came to be called the *Moho* in honor of Mohorovičić . It forms the major division that separates the crust above from denser mantle rock below.

Outer Core and Inner Core

In 1906, the British geologist R. D. Oldham announced that Earth had a core, a central region similar to the yolk of an egg. He was studying the travel paths of P-waves from earthquakes as they passed through the planet. Instead of following a straight-line path, at one point they were suddenly bent off course and formed a "shadow zone." Imagine an earthquake with its focus at the North Pole, as shown in the diagram. P-waves speed outward in all directions from the focus, but as they strike some denser material deep within Earth they are bounced off course in a new direction, like a billiard ball bouncing off the cushion of a pool table. The result is a shadow zone nearly empty of P-waves. So the new boundary marked the edge of a central core of some sort. The size of the core was worked out around 1940 by Beno Gutenberg of the California Institute of Technology. He put the core's outer edge at 1,800 miles (2,897 kilometers) beneath Earth's surface. But what was the core made of?

The next discovery helped answer that question. S-waves were not

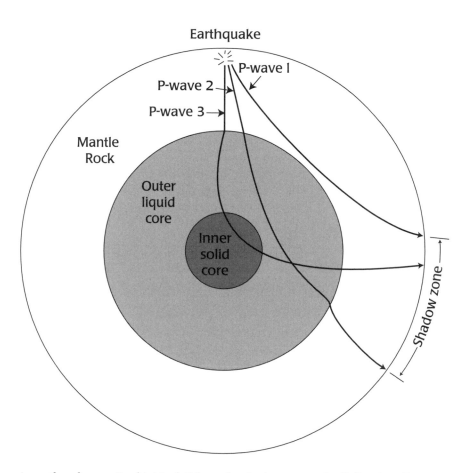

Earthquake

P-wave I

P-wave 2

P-wave 3

Mantle
Rock

Outer
liquid
core

Inner
solid
core

Shadow zone

An earthquake near Earth's North Pole sends seismic waves out in all directions. P-wave 1 misses striking the outer core and reaches Earth's surface. P-wave 2 strikes the outer core, is bent as it passes through it, and is bent again when it exits the outer core and reaches Earth's surface. The mantle region between P-waves 1 and 2 is called the shadow zone. The discovery that some P-waves were being bent into the shadow zone (P-wave 3) suggested that a solid inner core was contained within the outer liquid core.

entering the newfound core; or if they were, they were too weak to be detected. Since S-waves cannot pass through liquids, could that core be some kind of molten material? The answer seemed to be yes.

P-waves were bent off their straight course by the outer boundary of the core; then they were bent even more sharply by another boundary within the core. This showed there was yet another layer even deeper down. Also, the waves passing into this inner core of matter were speeded to much greater velocities than when traveling through the outer part of the core. This increase in velocity suggested a still denser and more rigid material.

The Danish seismologist I. Lehmann began studying the few P-waves that sometimes did manage to enter the shadow zone. How were they getting through? She concluded that deep within the molten core there must be a smaller, solid core that speeded up the P-waves and bent them so sharply that they skipped right into the shadow zone. Another scientist, Harold Jeffreys in England, agreed with Lehmann's findings and figured that the inner solid core was a rigid sphere 1,600 miles (2,575 kilometers) across. The picture of Earth's interior then seemed fairly complete.

We walk on a thin, solid rocky crust some 20 miles (32 kilometers) deep. Below is the plastic mantle of denser rock, to a depth of about 1,800 miles (2,897 kilometers). And at the center is Earth's core of even denser material, a ball within a ball—an outer core of liquid iron and nickel reaching down to about 3,100 miles (4,989 kilometers) and an inner core of solid iron and nickel, the center of which is 3,957 miles (6,368 kilometers) beneath the surface.

We have evidence other than that of P-waves for thinking that the planet's core is composed mostly of iron, along with some of the metallic element nickel. But there are bound to be new discoveries about the planet's interior as geologists continue to investigate with new instruments and advanced technology.

Earth as a Magnet

For many years, scientists have known that our planet is a giant magnet. Even ancient mariners used this natural magnetism to travel great distances across the oceans out of sight of land. Like a simple bar magnet, Earth has north and south magnetic poles that direct the motion of compass needles. The north-pole needle end of a compass always lines up with Earth's north magnetic pole. While scientists have known for years that Earth is a magnet, they have struggled to explain the hows and whys of its magnetism. They have little doubt that the secrets lie deep inside our planet.

One of the puzzling things about Earth as a magnet is that its magnetism seems to change over the years and centuries. Not only does it change in strength at any one location over time, but the planet's north magnetic pole wanders about, as shown in the diagram. For example, in the year 1912 the pole was located at 71 degrees north and 97 degrees west. But by 1942 it had shifted to 73 degrees north and 98 degrees west. Not only does the north magnetic pole wander about the Arctic, but in ages past the north and south magnetic poles have exchanged places—not once, but hundreds of times over the past tens of millions of years. It is not that the planet has flipped over, but that the magnetic poles have flipped positions. It is as if someone had removed a giant bar magnet from Earth's interior and reinserted it upside down.

The planet's magnetic field is thought to be created by strong movements of the molten iron and nickel in the liquid outer core. Earth's magnetic field is similar to that surrounding a bar magnet.

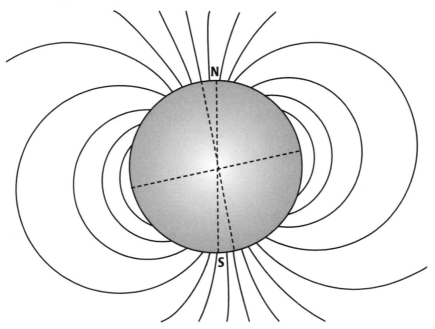

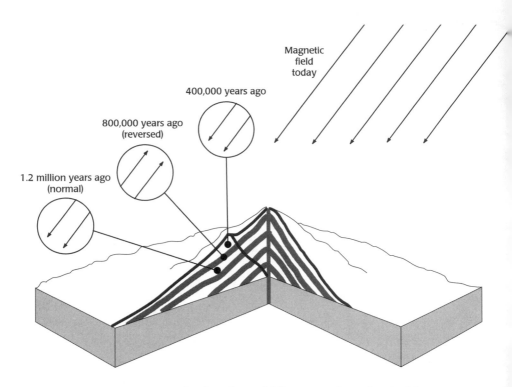

Ancient magnetism preserved in lava flows of different ages shows that Earth's magnetic field has flip-flopped several times. For example, long arrows show the direction of Earth's "normal" magnetic field today, with the north magnetic pole at the "top" of the planet. Four hundred thousand years ago the field also was normal; but 800,000 years ago it flipped to the opposite direction; 1.2 million years ago it was "normal."

These polar puzzles are not easy to figure out, nor is the main question underlying all studies of Earth's magnetism. But let's backtrack for a moment to review the work of the brilliant English scientist William Gilbert, who has been called the "Galileo of magnetism," then look at some present thinking to account for Earth's magnetism.

In 1600, Gilbert published *De magnete*, a book that excited the scientific community of his day. In it he said that Earth is a giant magnet that influences compass needles. He also made it clear that a line drawn from true north to true south formed the axis about which Earth spins like a top. Furthermore, this axis of rotation, he said, should not be confused with the axis resulting from a line connecting the magnetic north and magnetic south poles. The two north and two south polar points are quite different, he maintained.

Gilbert's major contribution at this stage, however, was his tracing of Earth's magnetic field. He began his experiments by cutting a piece of naturally magnetized mineral called loadstone into a sphere shaped like the planet. Then by moving small magnetic needles over the loadstone sphere he was able to trace the loadstone's lines of force. His conclusion was a simple one: Like the loadstone, Earth is a magnet, with similar lines of force. But what makes it a magnet? Gilbert suspected that Earth's overall magnetic field was produced by a large and permanent magnetic body deep inside. However, when later scientists learned that Earth's deep interior is very hot, the idea of a permanent magnetic body was given up. Any magnet heated to the temperature of Earth's deep interior quickly loses its magnetism. Nevertheless, Gilbert's contribution was an outstanding one. Before his experiments were published, no one understood the nature of Earth's magnetic field of force.

Gilbert's experiments dealt with what scientists today call Earth's primary magnetism. Even before Gilbert published *De magnete*, however, experimenters knew of secondary, or residual, magnetic forces that interfere with the planet's primary field. In the year 1580, for instance, observations made in London, England, showed that the compass needle pointed 11 degrees east of true north. Then the needle for some reason reversed its direction, until in 1812 it had "swung" to 24 degrees west of true north. Since that year it has been gradually shifting back toward the east. Today it points about only 10 degrees west of true north.

Scientists have long tried to predict or work out a cycle for these secondary changes, but to date they have had little luck. One reason is that a scant four hundred years of measurements in only a few locations is hardly enough to go on. If they had records going back a few thousand years, made at properly selected recording stations around the globe, they would be much better off. Also, without a clear understanding of what forces within the planet produce these secondary changes, they are greatly handicapped. Nevertheless, some scientists suspect that the residual field may be working its way around the globe in a westward direction. The drift has been steadily westward for centuries of observation. At its present rate of movement, the field seems to complete one full circle around the globe in about sixteen hundred years.

What Magnetized the Planet?

Is it possible that the planet's metal central region *is* capable of being magnetized, despite the great heat there? Some physicists feel that the extremely high pressure in the core region may offset the high-temperature effects and so permit magnetized material to exist there. Unhappily, this idea cannot be proved or disproved because in the laboratory we cannot produce pressures as high as nature produces within the planet.

Another attempt to explain Earth's magnetic field is called the *dynamo* theory, proposed by the British physicists Walter M. Elsasser and Edward Bullard. It holds that electric currents are generated by the flow of molten iron-nickel material that makes up the core region. These currents in turn set up the primary magnetic field that invisibly laces the globe. We can compare Earth as a dynamo with Michael Faraday's simple disk dynamo. Faraday was an English scientist who lived in the 1800s.

Faraday's dynamo consists of nothing more than a copper disk that spins above a bar magnet placed just under the edge of the disk. As the spinning disk passes through the field of the magnet, a small electric current is set up in the disk. By continuously spinning the disk, we can keep a current flowing, as shown in the diagram. This, then, is the dynamo principle: Mechanical energy (spinning of the disk) is changed into electrical energy (current).

Now let's look at our planet as a dynamo. Earth's core seems to be just the kind of material that a Faraday-type dynamo requires. Its iron-nickel is a good carrier of electricity, as is the copper wiring in your home. And since the outer core is liquid, the iron-nickel mix can move about. In short, since it allows both mechanical motion and the flow of a current, the combined effect of the two can generate currents and magnetism that just keep going on and on and on by themselves. That the core matter is in motion can't be denied. If it were not, then why would we notice changes in the planet's magnetic field? If the core were stable and motionless, the magnetic field probably would remain steady.

Now we are faced with the question, What causes the liquid iron-nickel core to be in motion? (The motion doesn't seem to be very fast, possibly only 3 feet (0.9 meter) an hour, but a dynamo the size of Earth doesn't have to turn very fast to produce a flow of current.) One answer is that heat is flowing outward from the core. This would set up convection currents similar to those in a pan of boiling water. Another possible answer is this: Differences in chemical make-up within the core could cause the core's material to move about. This happens in the oceans when the salt content of neighboring patches of water differs. Whatever the cause of the motion, many electric currents in the form of eddies are set up within the core, and the eddies constantly change as movement within the core changes.

So the dynamo theory can account for local currents, but not for the planet's overall magnetic field. What, then, produces the more or less stable primary magnetic field with its lines of force looping from pole to pole, as if a great bar magnet were inside Earth? It now seems that Earth's rotation on its axis might line up the various local eddies and so produce the primary field. If not, Elsasser asks, then why is the primary field aligned with Earth's axis of rotation? Until a better idea comes along, the dynamo theory seems to work just fine to account for Earth's magnetic field.

Asthenosphere and Lithosphere

Is our picture of Earth's interior as described so far the final blueprint? Probably not. There have been some interesting recent discoveries about the ocean floor and about the pattern of volcanic activity under the oceans. Those discoveries suggest that Earth's first 450 miles (724 kilometers) from the surface downward are much more complex than Mohorovičić and those who came after him suspected.

One of the most important of these discoveries is a major subdivision of the upper mantle between the depths of 60 and 150 miles (97 and 241 kilometers). This important zone has been called the low-velocity zone. When P- and S-waves wiggle through this zone of the upper mantle, they slow down and do not speed up again until they leave the zone. This low-velocity zone, 90 miles (145 kilometers) thick, marks the beginning of a region of the upper mantle called the *asthenosphere*. The word comes from the Greek *asthenes*, meaning "without strength," and from the Greek *sphaira*, meaning "ball." The asthenosphere goes to a depth of about 450 miles (724 kilometers). Earthquakes do not occur beyond the base of the asthenosphere.

The asthenosphere behaves something like a white-hot poker, which can be reshaped by being pressed, or like a glacier, which can flow under pressure despite its rigidity. In much the same way, the asthenosphere responds to pressure by slowly flowing from one place to another. Uneven

Earthquake waves provide us with the way we picture the lithosphere and asthenosphere beneath. The crust and upper mantle make up the lithosphere. The asthenosphere lies beneath and begins with the low-velocity zone where the rock is partly melted. This soft region permits the lithosphere above to move about. The bottom of the asthenosphere is marked by the depth at which earthquakes no longer occur.

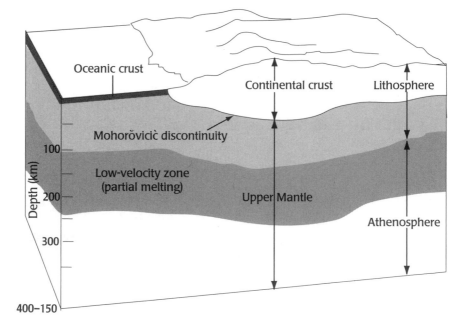

heating within the asthenosphere seems to be the energy source that drives this gradual movement. Although it is deep within the planet, this slow movement within the asthenosphere profoundly affects major surface features of our planet. Movement within the asthenosphere helps explain the drifting about of continents and spreading of the seafloor.

Above the asthenosphere, and extending up to the surface, is a zone called the *lithosphere*. The word comes from the Greek *lithos*, meaning "stone." Unlike the weak and mushy asthenosphere, the lithosphere is hard, rigid, stony, and strong. It includes the uppermost crustal layer of the planet, which was discovered by Mohorovičić . Interestingly, this crustal rock is not the same in the continents and the ocean floors.

The knowledge that continental rock differs from that of the ocean floors was one of the other important discoveries revealed by seismic studies. P-wave travel times are faster through the ocean floor's crustal rock than they are through the continental crust. Laboratory experiments have matched various kinds of rock with the speed of P-waves through them. On the basis of those experiments, as well as direct observation, we know that Earth's crustal rock under the continents is mostly the light-colored and relatively lightweight igneous rock called granite.

Until recently, geologists could only imagine the composition of the deep-oceanic crustal rock. That rock floor lies beneath more than 2 miles (3 kilometers) of seawater and thousands of feet (meters) of sediments. Ships with drilling rigs have dug into the seafloor and brought up rock core samples for examination. Other samples of deep oceanic floor rock well up out of volcanic islands such as Hawaii, and they erupt principally one kind of rock. By bringing all such evidence together, we found out that the oceanic rock floor is made up of a dark and heavy igneous rock called basalt.

Pressure and Temperature

Just as we cannot directly sample the rock of Earth's deep interior, we cannot directly measure the pressure and temperature profiles all the way down through the crust, then through the mantle, and finally into the central core.

Still, estimates of the deep pressures are not too difficult to come by. Below the lithosphere, pressure is determined by the thickness and density of the overlying rock at any point. We find out about density from the travel times of P-waves through the rock. The picture is that the denser the material, the deeper it must be. In the inner core, maximum pressure is more than 3.5 million times the atmospheric pressure at the surface.

Internal temperatures are harder to find out about. Temperature does not increase predictably with the thickness of the overlying rock. If we used as our guide the temperature increase of about 100 degrees Fahrenheit (38 degrees Centigrade) for each mile (1.6 kilometer) of depth in deep mines, then the temperature at the base of the mantle would have to be about 37,000 degrees Fahrenheit (20,537 degrees Centigrade). With such an increase it would be impossible for rocks to remain solid, or even liquid at such temperature and pressure. The actual temperatures at the bottom of the mantle must be much lower. Beyond these few ideas about conditions at these great depths, very little else can be said. However, recent estimates by the British physicist Francis Simon put the temperature at the boundary of the outer core and mantle at some 5,432 degrees Fahrenheit (3,000 degrees Centigrade). The temperature at the boundary of the outer and inner cores may rise to some 7,232 degrees Fahrenheit (4,000 degrees Centigrade), and the temperature at Earth's center may be some 7,412 degrees Fahrenheit (4,100 degrees Centigrade).

Our planet does not reveal information about its internal conditions willingly. It is only over the past two hundred years or so that the inventive genius of science and technology has gradually coaxed and pried out some of that information. And we will continue to work at it for centuries to come.

5

Restless Earth

If Earth were an apple, the thin skin would be Earth's solid-rock crust and the rigid upper-mantle rock just beneath. That 20-mile-deep (32-kilometer) "skin" of rock supports the planet's mountains, the massive pyramids of Egypt, and New York City's World Trade Center towers, and it acts as gigantic bathtubs for the world's oceans.

Wegener and Continental Drift

As solid, unmoving, and permanent as our planet's crust and upper-mantle rock seem, they are none of those things. Not until the 1960s and 1970s did most geologists come to accept an idea first proposed in 1912 by the German meteorologist Alfred Wegener. The continents wander, he said. As evidence, he pointed out that the eastern edge of South America forms a nice fit with the western edge of Africa, indicating that the two continents were once joined and later split apart. Since Wegener's time, geologists have provided overwhelming evidence for the drifting apart of those two, and other, continents. For example, they have shown that rocks of the two continents' edges were formed at the same time and in the same way.

Wegener's idea was to revolutionize geology. Most scientists of the time generally agreed that the continents may once have been connected. But they found it hard to explain how continents were able actually to drift apart and become separated by hundreds or thousands of miles of open

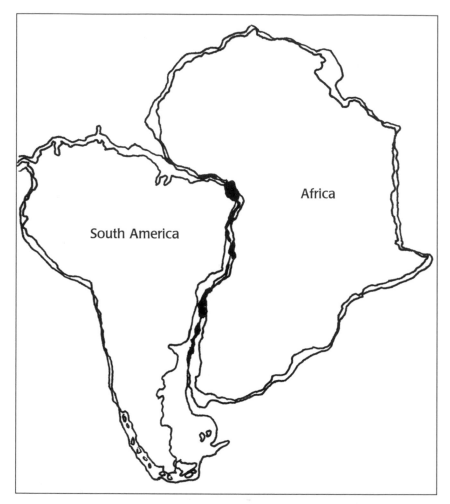

At a depth of about 3,000 feet (900 meters), the edges of South America and Africa fit snugly together. This suggested to the German meteorologist Alfred Wegener that the continents have drifted about over time. The dark spots in the diagram indicate areas where continental blocks overlap.

ocean, such as North America and Europe. The physical mechanisms allowing continents to move could not be found. So Wegener's idea, known as "continental drift," remained controversial.

As the ability to understand the behavior of earthquake shock waves improved, so did an understanding of Earth's interior. Could it be that Earth's lithosphere was made up of a number of giant *plates*, or rafts of solid rock? And could it be that those rafts move about on an enormous subterranean sea of puttylike rock, the asthenosphere? Today, the new science of plate tectonics, which grew out of Wegener's early idea, cannot be denied. There simply is too much evidence to support it.

The planet's crustal plates come in two general sizes. There are six large ones and about a dozen smaller ones arranged like pieces of a jigsaw puzzle. All move about slowly, on the average about as fast as your finger-nails grow. While some move less than .5 inch (1 centimeter) a year, others speed along at 3.5 inches (9 centimeters) a year. Whether slow or fast, plate movement continually shapes and reshapes the planet's land-forms and seas. It stretches the ocean basins and so enlarges them, or it compresses and shrinks them, over hundreds of thousands of years. Plate motion also triggers earthquakes, causes volcanoes to spout and spill out red-hot rock, and builds mountains along the plates' edges where they butt up against each other. Over longer periods—several hundred million years—plate movement has broken up giant continents into smaller ones, smashed other continents together, and always keeps the continents on the move. All such activity is created within the top 125 miles (200 kilo-meters) or so of Earth's restless skin.

Plates Move in Three Ways

There are three types of plate movement, and each produces its own effects at Earth's surface, whether on land or on the seafloor. One way is for two neighboring plates to pull away from each other. This is just what is happening to the South American Plate and the African Plate. As the South American Plate creeps westward, the African Plate creeps eastward. If two plates are pulling apart from each other, the cause can be that some-thing is *pushing* them apart along their common border. That cause is well known. It is a great crack along the floor of the Atlantic Ocean called the Midatlantic Ridge. The crack actually is a long chain of undersea volcanic mountains that snake their way some 43,000 miles (69,000 kilometers) along the ocean floor from the North Atlantic Ocean southward nearly to Antarctica.

All along the ridge is a *rift valley* formed by the tearing apart of the lithosphere. Magma welling upward out of the mantle produces hundreds of volcanoes along the edges of the rift valley. This outpouring of lava seems to be pushing the two large plates away from each other. The result is *seafloor spreading*, in this case a widening of the Atlantic Ocean. If a continent or other large landmass happens to be sitting on top of such a ridge of upwelling mantle rock, the landmass is broken apart. Today, that is just what is happening to Iceland and, on a much larger scale, to the eastern third of Africa. Two branches of a several-thousand-mile-long rift valley, known as the Rift Valley, run almost the length of the African continent. In the past, the Gulf of California was formed in this way, as was the Red Sea. We will have more to say about these mid-ocean ridges in chapter 8.

As two plates are pushed apart by volcanic outpourings along a rift valley, what happens to their opposite edges? One result is what is happening along the westward forward edge of the South American Plate. As the diagram shows, the forward edge is being pushed into the forward edge of the neighboring Nazca Plate. The Nazca Plate also is doing some pushing, since it is being moved eastward by outpourings of volcanic rock from a second major rift valley called the East Pacific Rise.

What happens when two such giant plates collide? At the surface, in the case of the South American and Nazca Plates, there are lots of volcanoes, lots of earthquakes, and lots of mountain building along the common edge where the two plates meet. That is just how the mighty Andes mountain range, which runs the length of the western edge of South America, was formed.

But something even more interesting happens deep down at the common edge of the colliding plates. In our example here, the westward edge of the lightweight continental rock of the South American Plate is riding up over the eastward edge of the heavyweight basaltic rock of the Nazca Plate. This shoves the leading edge of the Nazca Plate down into the upper mantle as what geologists call a *subduction zone*. As the plate edge is forced down, it pulls part of the basaltic ocean-floor crust down

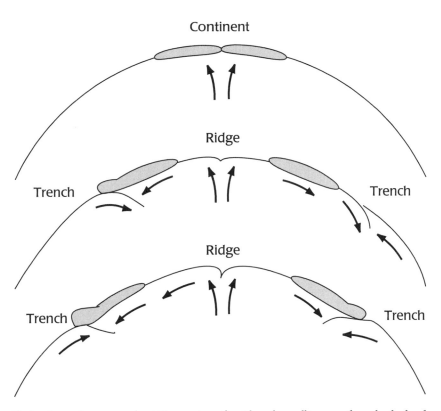

Continent

Ridge

Trench

Trench

Ridge

Trench

Trench

If a landmass happens to be sitting on top of a ridge of upwelling mantle rock, the land-mass will be split apart. This is just what is happening to Iceland, which sits on top of the Midatlantic Ridge.

with it. The result is the formation of a deep oceanic trench—the Peru-Chile Trench—along the western shores of South America. As the forward edge of the Nazca Plate is bent and pushed down into the mantle, it is heated so much that some melts. This newly melted rock then forces its way up through the South American Plate. From time to time the fluid rock boils up to the surface and spills over the surrounding land as volcanic outpourings that help form the Andes Mountains.

How else may plates move, collide, separate and so change Earth's surface features? One way is for two plates to rub together as they slide and grind past each other. The zone of contact may run for a few to hundreds of miles or kilometers, depending on the size of the plates. Such contact between plates produces a rupture line of crustal rock called a fault line. California's famous San Andreas Fault is an example and marks the common border of the North American and Pacific Plates. Year after year, as the two plates push and grind against each other along a fault line, friction causes the rock along each plate edge to stretch rather than slip freely. Eventually, the rock faces along the contact zone reach their limit of stretching. When they do, they snap along the fault line and dishes begin to fall off shelves.

What Causes Plate Movement?

Even though geologists can measure what Earth's plates are doing, they have yet to come up with an explanation that everyone agrees on. One theory of plate movement suggests that the plates move because they are being pulled along by the action of their leading edge diving downward into the mantle. At the same time, along their opposite trailing edge thousands of miles away, the plates are being pushed apart and shoved along by upwelling magma along the rift valleys. We can compare the action with that of a department store escalator. The stairs, and people on them, are carried along until the stairs dip down out of sight at the top. (Usually, the people are smart enough to step off!) The stairs then upwell from the bottom and, along with a new group of people, are once again carried along. If plates move along in a similar way, then we must ask what it is that drives seafloor spreading (the push) at one end and plate diving (the pull) at the opposite edge.

Most geologists today look to something called the *convection cell* theory. They see the rift valleys of the Pacific and Atlantic oceans as lying along a rising convection current. Heat deep within the mantle produces conveyor-belt motion of neighboring cells, or compartments, of molten rock. Where two neighboring cells turning in opposite directions meet, they push molten rock upward and out onto the ocean floor. This action creates the rift valley and keeps feeding it with new outpourings of lava. It is that action of the convection cells that seems to drive seafloor spreading, which in turn may be keeping the plates moving. But there may be another driving force in the upper mantle rock.

Some geologists look to the *plume* theory. They think that hot rock in certain places of the lower mantle rises into the upper mantle rock as broad areas called *hot spots*. Over the past ten million years, some one hundred twenty hot spots have been active, according to one study, but only twenty seem to be active now. When a plume rises into the upper mantle, it fans out to cover an area a few hundred miles across. Each of the twenty major hot-spot plumes around the world creates a zone of volcanic activity. Outside the region of a plume's hot, rising rock is a region of cooler mantle rock that is being sucked down to replace the rising rock. In this way convection cells are formed. Is this actually the driving force of convection cells? No one knows. We will have more to say about the plume theory and hot spots in the chapter about the ocean floor.

Geologists can tell that plate movements have been the rule for at least the past billion years. Even so, they have to do a lot more research before they gain a solid understanding of the interaction of forces that moves the plates.

Plate Movement and the Future

Plate movements have brought dramatic changes to landforms and life-forms throughout much of geologic history; they will keep doing so for another billion years, and more. Plant and animal fossils found in Antarctica show that that great landmass has not always been anchored at the South Pole, but at an earlier time was located closer to the Equator, in a climate zone more favorable for palm trees than for penguins.

We now know that Earth's many environmental zones are ever changing, and that a major part of that change is brought about by plate movement. As the continents continue to glide across the face of our planet, they contribute to climatic change. Mountain chains are thrust up in one place by plate movement while ocean trenches some 6 miles (9.6 kilometers) deep are sucked down nearby.

As plate tectonics has altered the land and the oceans, so has plate movement altered the life-forms of land and marine ecosystems. Over hundreds of thousands of years, the ocean basins have expanded, contracted, and expanded again. Fifty million years from now, the Mediterranean Sea is scheduled to shrink to the size of a large lake and the Red Sea to open into a wider ocean. In ages past, much of the planet's water has been locked up as ice that covered broad expanses of the Northern Hemisphere. Sea level was much lower then. One result was changes in ocean chemistry and circulation patterns, which in turn determined which ocean-dwelling animal and plant species would survive, and which would not.

Old supercontinents have broken up, reformed, and broken up again, as they will keep doing. In the process, habitats and continental climates have changed. As the great ice sheets come and go, sea level rises or lowers by some 300 feet (91 meters). All such changes cause or nudge the biological processes associated with mass extinctions. The mass extinctions in turn open the floodgate of evolution of new species and an explosion of biodiversity results. The new species, and existing species that had long been waiting for a change that would favor them, thrive amid the new conditions.

Fifty million years from now, plate movement is expected to break Africa apart. And one day part of California will be broken away and shoved northward toward the Aleutian Islands. In that distant future, today's biology and geography books will be historical curiosities.

6

Weather, Climate, and Great Ice

Of the three large physical features of planet Earth—the land, oceans, and air—it is the dynamics of the atmosphere that most affects our daily lives. The cocoon of atmosphere not only encloses you in a pressure chamber that prevents your body from exploding, but it also provides the oxygen fuel needed for your body to function as a complex chemical machine. Driven by energy from the Sun, the atmosphere's global circulation heats us, freezes us, batters us with violent storms, and provides the most popular topic of conversation—the weather, and its long-term version, climate.

Our Ocean of Air

We can imagine ourselves as living on the floor of an ocean of air. At the bottom we are safe and comfortable, but drawn up near the top we would die, like a fish drawn up out of water. Held captive by Earth's gravity, our ocean of air surrounds the planet to a depth of hundreds of miles, or kilometers. But 99 percent of the atmosphere is compressed into a layer about 20 miles (32 kilometers) deep.

Remove the atmosphere and there would be no trees, no animals, no clouds, and no sound. Ours would be a dead planet like Mercury or like the Moon. By day the direct rays of the Sun would heat everything to above the boiling point of water. By night temperatures would plunge a

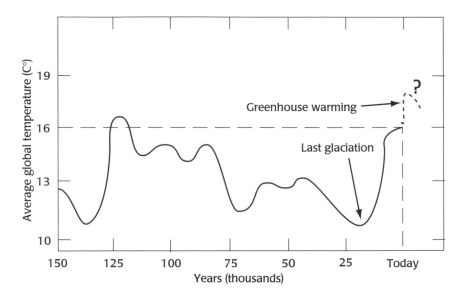

The ups and downs of global warming and chilling are shown for the past 150,000 years. Where global warming will take us over the next 50 years or so is a big question mark. It could lead to the hottest times in recorded history. A global temperature change of less than ten degrees marks the difference between an ice age and warmer periods.
AFTER J. M. MITCHELL JR.

few hundred degrees below the freezing point. As a greenhouse provides heat to its plants, our atmosphere serves as a blanket that prevents much of Earth's stored heat from radiating away into space.

The atmosphere is a mixture of gases, dust, and other material. Most of the air (78 percent) is nitrogen, an element that is important as a food for plants but that we do not use directly. Most of the remaining gas (21 percent) is oxygen, which nearly all of Earth's organisms depend on for life. One percent is a mixture of water vapor, argon, helium, neon, ozone, carbon dioxide, salt from the oceans, dust from volcanoes and meteors, bits and pieces of rocks and sand, pollen from plants, and still other substances.

We can picture the atmosphere as a tall stack of feather pillows. The weight of the higher pillows compresses the lower ones. This results in greater pressure being exerted on the lower pillows. That is why the air pressure at ground level is greater than the pressure at higher altitudes, and why high-flying aircraft have to pressurize their cabins. At sea level, the air presses in on your body with a force of 14.7 pounds per square inch (6.67 kilograms per square centimeter) of body surface.

We can further imagine the atmosphere as being made up of layers, each layer having its own pressure and temperature oddities that make it different from the other layers.

The first and lowest layer of air is the *troposphere*. It is the densest layer and is where almost all of our weather takes place. Over the United States, the troposphere reaches to a height of about 40,000 feet (12,192 meters), or nearly 8 miles (13 kilometers). On a hot August day, the air temperature at the bottom of the troposphere may be 95 degrees Fahrenheit (35 degrees Centigrade), but at the top it will be –70 degrees Fahrenheit (–57 degrees Centigrade). The temperature of this air layer falls off at an average rate of 3.5 degrees Fahrenheit for every 1,000 feet (6 degrees Centigrade for every 1,000 meters). The cooling with increased altitude is due to radiant heat given off by the ground, which warms the air next to the ground more than it warms the air higher up.

The second air layer, the *stratosphere*, begins wherever the troposphere ends and goes up to a height of about 30 miles (48 kilometers). Like the upper troposphere, the lower stratosphere is swept with strong winds and is extremely cold. Higher up, however, the winds die and the temperature gradually rises, reaching 30 degrees Fahrenheit (–1 degree Centigrade) at the top. The cause of this sudden warming is a layer of the gas ozone, which is a form of oxygen that contains three atoms. The oxygen we breathe contains two atoms. The *ozone layer* blocks out most of the high-energy *ultraviolet radiation* from the Sun. Without the protective ozone layer, living organisms exposed to the full force of that damaging radiation would be seriously harmed. Atmospheric pressure at the top of the stratosphere is only 1/1,000 the pressure at sea level, which makes it almost the same as being in deep space.

Resting on top of the stratosphere is the *mesosphere*, an air layer about 20 miles (32 kilometers) deep. The temperature continues to fall with height into the mesosphere, reaching about –130 degrees Fahrenheit (–90 degrees Centigrade) near the top. At this altitude the air has so few molecules to scatter light that the sky is nearly black.

Topping the mesosphere is the fourth major air layer: the *thermosphere*. It marks the borderline with space and extends to a height of more than 20,000 miles (32,186 kilometers). Since there are so very few gas molecules at thermosphere altitudes, there is no transfer of heat from the air to any object in the air. Any living creature taken up into the thermosphere and exposed would perish by being broiled to death on the side facing the Sun and frozen to death on the side in shadow.

The Atmosphere in Motion

Our planet's air is kept in continuous motion by energy from the Sun and by Earth's rotation on its axis. Many local effects on the ground also keep the air in motion. They include air masses moving about, the wind, and vertical air currents driven aloft by the heat boiling off a field on a hot summer day.

The major wind systems that account for the general circulation of air around the globe occur in seven belts, as shown in the diagram. We count the Equator as one belt. In addition, there are three belts in the Northern Hemisphere and three in the Southern Hemisphere.

Throughout the year, the Sun's energy falls most intensely on a broad belt that extends just northward and southward of the Equator. All along the sunlit section of this belt, over land and sea alike, Earth's surface and the air above it are heated. The heating expands the air and so sets up a low-pressure system of rising air.

Much the same thing happens above a living-room radiator. Heat from the radiator causes the air just above to expand and rise, setting up a local low-pressure system in one part of the living room. As the Equator's low-pressure system of air rises to great heights, the air is cooled, becomes heavy, and tends to sink back to the ground again. But a steady flow of hot, rising air pushing up from below prevents it from doing so. That hot, rising air is laden with moisture in the form of water vapor, which is water in the form of a gas rather than a liquid. As it is cooled at a higher altitude, the water vapor condenses into clouds, and the cloud water droplets fall as rain, providing the land areas of the Equatorial belt with abundant rainfall.

The belt of air girdling the Equator is carried along at the rotational speed of Earth's surface at the Equator. That speed is about 1,000 miles (1,609 kilometers) an hour. So, relative to the Equatorial belt, the air above the Equator has very little motion, except for its upward motion. What little wind blows is usually light and variable, and those parts of the Equatorial belt of air that lie over the oceans are often dead calm. Masters of those grand sailing ships of old dreaded this part of the ocean. For days on end, they found themselves becalmed under the blistering tropical Sun. They called this belt of calm the *doldrums*.

As the Equatorial air rises aloft, some of it streams northward toward the North Pole while some of it streams southward toward the South Pole. At about 30 degrees north and south latitudes, some of the air curves downward toward the surface. It tends to pile up and form a high-pressure system called the *horse latitudes*. Similar to the doldrums, the horse latitudes becalmed sailing ships and their cargoes of horses for days on end, sometimes for so long that the horses had to be eaten or thrown overboard to save drinking water. In general, the air here is fairly calm, or if there are winds they are light and variable. The climate of the horse latitudes is generally sunny, hot, and dry. Some of the world's great modern-day desert areas—northern Mexico, northern Africa, and northern India—lie along this belt.

The high-pressure air at the horse latitudes doubles back and flows close to the surface toward the Equator, replacing the Equatorial air that rises aloft. This outward-flowing air forms a broad belt of wind called the *trade winds*, which blow rather steadily. Because this air is not keeping pace with Earth's rotational speed at this latitude, the trade winds blow at a slant instead of looping straight back to the Equator. In the Northern Hemisphere, they blow from northeast to southwest and are called the northeast trades. In the Southern Hemisphere, they blow from the southeast to the northwest and are called the southeast trades. This slanting effect caused by Earth's rotation is called the *Coriolis effect*. The slant of the trade winds also affects the course of ocean currents, as you will find in the next chapter.

From about 35 degrees north and south latitudes to about 55 degrees is another wind belt, called the *prevailing westerlies*. In the Northern Hemisphere it blows from southwest to northeast. In the Southern Hemisphere it blows from northwest to southeast. The air that forms this wind belt has its source in the mainstream of air flowing northward and southward from the Equator. In the latitude of the westerlies, this air moves faster than Earth's rotational speed; so, like the trade winds, the westerlies blow at a slant, but in the opposite direction. That is, these winds blow out of the south and toward the north in the Northern Hemisphere, and out of the north and toward the south in the Southern Hemisphere.

Like the trade winds, the westerlies blow steadily day and night at Earth's surface. But they are strongest aloft, and we feel their effect most at altitudes where the airliners fly. A plane eastward bound from New York to Europe is carried along by the westerlies, or *jet stream*, and it can make the trip in about two hours less time than it can on the return flight, against the winds, from Europe to New York.

Mountains, valleys, plains, and other features of Earth's surface interfere with the flow of the westerlies at ground level. That is one reason that we do not feel their steady force at the surface. Warm, moist air moving up from the south and cold, dry air moving down from the north meet in the path of the westerlies. This contributes to the ever-changing winds and variety of storms that make the westerlies our most active weather belt. Whenever the path of the westerlies over certain regions of Earth changes temporarily, marked changes in weather occur. It seems likely that Indians of the American Southwest abandoned their farmlands over a period of two centuries, from A.D. 1200 to A.D. 1400, as a result of a long-term shift of the westerlies that brought extended drought. The cliff-dwelling Indians of Mesa Verde, Colorado, ran away or perished during the years 1271 to 1285. The once-proud Mycenean civilization of ancient Greece three thousand years ago also seems to have been dried up by extended drought brought by the shifting westerlies.

Some of the hot, moist air that begins its poleward journey from the Equator reaches the polar ice caps. By the time it arrives at the top and bottom of the world, however, it has been cooled and nearly drained of its moisture. This air tends to pile up at the poles, where it forms high-

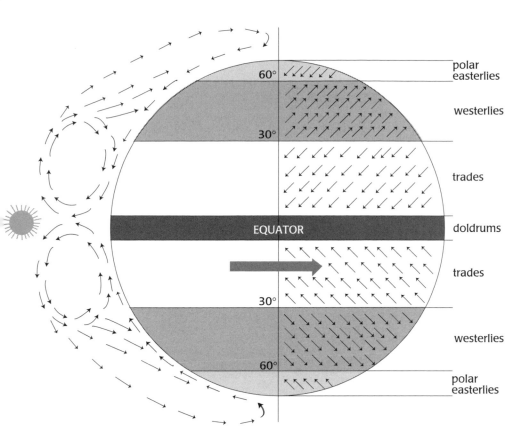

Earth's atmosphere is set in motion by energy from the Sun. Large belts of global circulation of the air are kept in motion, as shown. The air cells are moved on a slant, rather than north and south, by the effects of the planet's rotation on its axis.

pressure caps. Because the speed of this air is slower than Earth's rotational speed at these high latitudes, the *polar easterlies*, as they are called, blow in the same slanting direction as the trade winds. That is, they are northerly winds at the surface in the Northern Hemisphere and southerly winds in the Southern Hemisphere.

These, then, are the major wind systems girdling Earth and regulating its weather, climate, and human activity. They are described as "ideal" systems. We have not considered the many variations of mountains and other features, the seasons, and the oceans, all of which tend to disrupt the neat profile just drawn.

Earth's Changing Seasons

Earth's orbital path around the Sun is not a perfect circle, but an ellipse. Its elliptical orbit positions Earth somewhat closer to the Sun at certain times and somewhat farther away at other times. Many people think that our distance from the Sun is least in summer and greatest in winter. Actually, it is just the opposite. We are closest to the Sun in January and most distant in July. Then why isn't it hotter in winter and cooler in summer?

The cause of the seasons lies not in Earth's distance from the Sun but in the way it faces the Sun. As the diagram shows, Earth is tilted a bit in space, at an angle of 23.5 degrees, although the amount of tilt varies by about 3 degrees over long periods of time. A tilted Earth means that the Sun's rays strike North America, for example, at different angles—and so with different intensities—at different times of the year depending on where Earth happens to be in its orbit.

As winter gives way to spring and spring to summer, each day the noontime Sun appears a bit higher in the sky than on the previous day. Because of the Sun's higher overhead position and because the days gradually lengthen, each day grows a little warmer. It is warmer because the Sun's rays strike us from more directly overhead than before. Then as summer gives way to fall and fall to winter, each day becomes a bit shorter, the noontime Sun appears a bit lower in the sky, and the air grows a little cooler.

In the Northern Hemisphere, summer begins about June 22, at which time the noontime Sun appears at its highest point in the sky. That marks the official beginning of summer and is the day when we in the Northern Hemisphere have the greatest number of daylight hours. After that, the days begin to grow shorter and the nights longer, until at official autumn, about September 21, day and night are of equal length.

Because Earth remains tilted in the same direction in space with respect to its orbit, the Northern Hemisphere tilts back away from the Sun over the next three months. South America now receives the rays of the Sun more directly and soon enjoys long summer days. When the Northern Hemisphere is tilted back in its farthest position, by about December 22, the noonday Sun reaches its lowest point in the sky. The Northern Hemisphere then receives the Sun's rays at the lowest angle, which means the least amount of heating. This first day of winter marks the shortest day of the year, after which the days grow increasingly longer as the Sun appears progressively higher in the sky each day.

Three months later, about March 21, the length of day and night are again equal, marking the arrival of spring. We continue to see the noonday Sun climb higher in the sky daily, and the days gradually grow warmer.

Earth has not always been tilted at an angle of 23.5 degrees, nor will it always be, because of a motion called *precession*. As the planet spins on its axis, it wobbles, as does a top that is running out of spin energy. The reason is that Earth is not a perfect sphere. Because it rotates on its axis, it has developed a slight bulge at the Equator and slight flattening at the poles. The diameter at the Equator is some 27 miles (43 kilometers) greater than the polar diameter. And because the Equator is tilted 23.5 degrees, the Sun's and Moon's gravitational tug on our planet are not in line with each other. What happens is that Earth's axis slowly gets twisted around in a circle, one circle being completed every 25,800 years. This means that the North Star, presently Polaris, is not always the same star. In 3000 B.C., for example, the star Thuban, in the constellation Draco, was the North Star. In the year A.D. 7000 it will be Aldermain, in the constellation Cepheus.

Climate Change

What have Earth's past climates been like, and what can we expect of the future? Climatologists have a number of ways of poking into ancient climates. One is the study of fossils. For example, lots of fossil remains of different kinds of reptiles discovered in a certain rock layer would tell us that the climate was characterized by warmth, not cold. Because reptiles are cold-blooded animals, meaning that they cannot regulate their body temperature, they must depend on the surrounding temperature to warm them. The climate at the time the reptiles lived and were fossilized, therefore, must have been warm. And so it was during the Mesozoic era, known as the Age of Reptiles.

The fatness or thinness of an ancient tree's annual growth rings provides another clue to past climates. In times of plenty of rain, the rings are fat and indicate rapid growth. In times of drought, they are thin and reveal slow growth. California's giant Sequoia trees reveal rainfall patterns over some four thousand years.

Ancient soils brought up in cores drilled from the ground also pry climate secrets out of the distant past. A soil core taken in Czechoslovakia showed a sequence of alternating warm and cool periods that spanned nearly a million years. One of the clues was the presence in certain of the soil layers of tiny snails known to be of a cold-dwelling kind. Climatologists have many other ways of reading our planet's climate history. A study of the fossilized oxygen found in tiny marine organisms that lived many millions of years ago reveals the temperature of ancient seas. The rise and fall of ancient seas, which can be read in ancient seabeds, provide a clue about our glacial history. A lowering of the mean sea level indicates that water was being removed to make glaciers. A rise indicates that glaciers were going through a stage of melting.

Great Ice

The past two million years of Earth's climate history have been interesting ones, cold ones. Several ice ages have come and gone. Over the last seven hundred thousand years, according to climatologist Reid A. Bryson, there have been seven ice ages that alternated with interglacial, warmer periods. It seems that we in the Northern Hemisphere may now be near the peak of such a warm, interglacial period and may be headed for another long-term deep freeze.

Studies suggest that each cycle of peak glacial activity—from one peak, then through an interglacial period, then to the peak of the next glacial period—lasts about 100,000 years. Interglacial periods, from the end of one glacial period to the beginning of the next, take about 10,000 years.

The peak of the last glacial period came about 18,000 years ago, and the period ended about 13,000 years ago. At the peak, ice covered about 30 percent of Earth's total land surface and was some 2 miles (3.2 kilometers) thick over parts of North America. While all that water was locked up on the land as ice, the world ocean level dropped about 330 to 460 feet (100 to 140 meters).

No one knows for certain what triggers an ice age, although there are several theories. All fall into one of two groups: 1) Ice ages are set off by astronomical conditions. For example, a decrease in energy output of the Sun from time to time; or the Solar System passing through a nebula, a large cloud of space dust and gas, which would lessen the amount of solar radiation reaching Earth; or variations in Earth's orbit that move the planet

Ice ages have come and gone many times in the planet's history. Many areas of the world today are still gripped in a glacial age. One example in the United States is the Yetna Glacier in Mount McKinley National Monument. The Mount Russel icefall can be seen entering from the left. NATIONAL PARKS SERVICE PHOTO BY NORMAN HERKENHAM

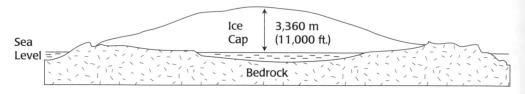

A leftover of the most recent ice age, which ended some ten thousand years ago, is the Greenland ice cap. Today the ice reaches a maximum depth of 11,000 feet (3,360 meters). If all that ice were spread evenly over Earth's surface, it would form a layer 17 feet (5 meters) thick.

closer and farther away from the Sun in known cycles; or changes in Earth's tilt due to precession. 2) Ice ages are set off by events on Earth itself. For example, ice ages may occur during times of extensive mountain building or increased volcanic activity. Or they occur as plate activity moves the continents about, in the process changing their elevation above sea level. Plate activity also changes the pattern of global air circulation and ocean currents. The ocean currents are important movers of heat from one part of the globe to another, as you will find in the next chapter. At our present stage of long-range climate forecasting, we have no hard answer, only hints, to Earth's next major climate change.

Then can we reliably say *anything* about Earth's future climate? Many climatologists look to Earth's known orbital variations as the main cause of long-term climate change. Orbital variations are something we can measure and predict, unlike the effects of mountain building. If climatologists who favor the orbital theory are right, then the long-term forecast over the next twenty thousand years or so seems to be toward cooling and increased glaciation in the Northern Hemisphere.

With each chapter, it becomes more evident that Earth is a planet characterized by change rather than by sameness.

7

Realm of the Oceans

A Bottomless Sea

For many hundreds of years, people ventured out onto the sea with great fear and caution, for what lay deep below was unknown. The unknown has often been a source of fear. As recently as the 1800s, some superstitious people thought that not far beyond the shores, the sea had no bottom. Others believed that when a ship sank, it remained suspended in the water forever. The reasoning was that the ocean became denser and denser with depth because of the great weight of the water above. So a ship, or any other object, would come to a stop about a mile (1.6 kilometers) down. Still other people believed that the seafloor—if there was one—would be found to be flat and featureless.

And there were dreaded, fearsome "monsters" of the deep. Tall tales of such beings are echoed in Rudyard Kipling's *Just So Stories*. In one, King Solomon planned to feed all the world's animals in a single day. When he had the food ready, one animal appeared from the sea and ate everything in one gulp. The animal explained ". . . I am the smallest of thirty thousand brothers, and our home is at the bottom of the sea . . . and where I come from we eat twice as much as that between meals." There were beliefs in "sea serpents," as well, most likely based on rare sightings of giant squid with tentacles 40 feet (12 meters) long.

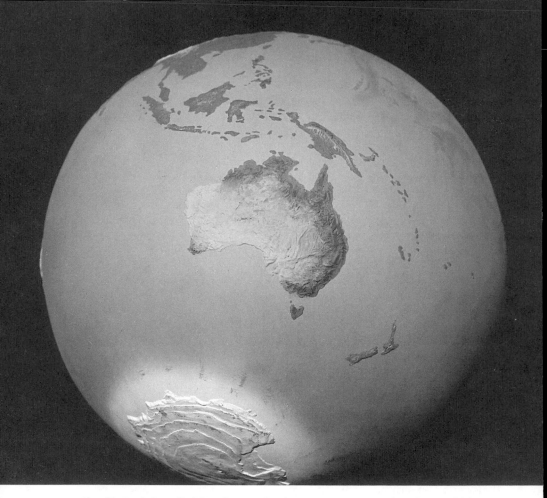

Should Earth be called "Sea" instead? If we were over Australia, this would be our view of the Pacific Ocean region of our planet. Its surface is 71 percent water, some 140 million square miles (361 million square kilometers) of it. On average, the ocean depth is about 3 miles (4.8 kilometers).

Origin and Makeup of the Oceans

Throughout Earth's long history, the sizes and shapes of its ocean basins have changed continuously, as they are changing today. As you found in chapter 2, the cooling of the planet's early crustal rock permitted the pooling of water, which was squeezed out of the solidifying lava and came from comets and rains. The pools overflowed as rivers, which over hundreds of thousands of years sought the lowest levels of the land and so flowed into basins to form the first seas.

Today most of Earth's surface—about 71 percent—is covered by some 140 million square miles (361 million square kilometers) of ocean water about 3 miles (4.8 kilometers) deep, on average. If the planet's mountains were scraped flat and its valleys filled in, the entire land surface would be flooded to a depth of about 2.5 miles (4 kilometers).

As the shapes and sizes of the ocean basins have changed over time, so has the chemistry of their water. Since the oceans first formed, they have been collecting mineral salts washed off the land and dissolved in the water. But the oceans are not very well stirred by their currents, waves, and tides, so we find differences in salinity from one part of an ocean to another and from shallow water to deep water. In general, ocean water that receives heavy rainfalls and ocean regions near the mouths of large rivers are the least salty. The main salt is sodium chloride, or common table salt. If you evaporated a pint of seawater, there would be about a teaspoonful of salt left in the jar.

Over the hundreds of millions of years since the oceans formed, they have been collecting more and more minerals and other materials. Among them are bromine, which we use to improve the quality of gasoline, and magnesium, a lightweight metal used in aircraft. In addition, almost all metals are found in the sea, including gold and silver. In fact, there is so much gold dissolved in seawater that a cubic mile (4.17 cubic kilometers) of water contains about a ton of the metal. That is what we would expect, knowing that the oceans have long been gathering materials from the weathering away of rocks and minerals on the land.

However, there is so much ocean water that its mineral concentrations build up very slowly. Wind-whipped ocean waves lose large amounts of salt to the air, as well. Still, there is enough salt in the world's seawater to cover the continents with a layer 5 feet (1.5 meters) deep. In fact, large areas of the continents are paved with the salts from ancient, dried-up oceans. Among them are the hard-as-cement salt flats found in Utah, for example. Some of the world's salt flats are up to 2,000 feet (610 meters) thick. Flats of salt and gypsum (a sulfate compound of calcium), for example, evaporated from seawater have formed many times in Earth's history. During the Silurian period, for instance, nearly 5,000 feet (1,500 meters) of sediments, nearly half of which is salt and gypsum, accumulated in what is today central Michigan.

Waves and How They Travel

If you ever watch waves breaking on the beach on a lazy summer day, you can learn much about their anatomy and motion. Waves are generated and driven by the wind. You can even learn something about waves by watching them move down the length of a swimming pool on a windy day. At the upwind end of the pool, the waves will be crowded, with only short distances between them. Farther along the pool, toward the downwind end, they will be separated by longer and longer distances.

The distance over which a train of waves runs is called the *fetch*. The longer the fetch, the longer and faster the waves. And the stronger the wind, the larger the waves build. Giant waves towering to 60 feet (18 meters) and crashing on the shores of Europe sometimes originate off the coast of the United States some 2,000 miles (3,219 kilometers) away. The long fetch is what speeds these waves along, stretches them out, and builds them to impressive heights.

The peak of a wave is called the *wave crest*, and the lowest point between two waves is the *wave trough*. The distance between two wave crests is the wave's length, and the length of time it takes two successive crests in a wave train to break over a rock, for instance, or some other fixed reference point is the *wave period*. Anyone who enjoys a little mental arithmetic can pass the time with the simple equation $P = L/S$, where P is the wave period, L its length, and S its speed. Suppose that you use a watch to get the wave period by counting off the seconds between wave crests breaking over a rock. Say that $P = 10$ seconds. Next you want to find L and S. You can find S by remembering that it is 5.14 times P in seconds. So S in our example is 5.14×10 (seconds), or 51.4 feet per second.

Now that you know P and S, you can find L by multiplying the square of P by 5.1. That amounts to 100×5.1, which equals 510 feet for the wavelength. If you did this little experiment many times, you would find that the speed of waves varies a lot and depends on wavelength.

Wavelength is what determines to what depth a wave's disturbance is felt. The rule is that the longer the wave, the deeper the disturbance. Some waves are so long that they disturb the water all the way down to the floor of the deepest oceans. In general, however, waves tend to disturb only the water close to the surface in the deep ocean. As waves move into shallow water, they make themselves felt along the rising bottom. A wave breaks onto the beach when its height from crest to trough becomes about

Diagrams show the anatomy of a wave and how the circular motion of the water beneath a wave simply causes a floating object to bob up and down beneath an ocean wave rather than being moved onto the shore by the wave. Notice the small amount of water movement at a depth one-half the wavelength.

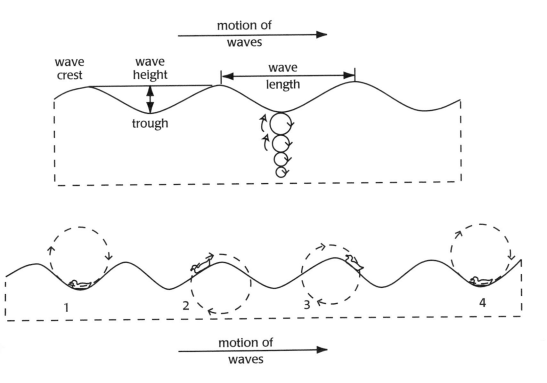

one and a half times the depth of the water. Not only does the wave break, but something else happens to it.

Many people think that the motion of a wave carries the water of the wave right along. That is not what happens. You can convince yourself by watching a seagull floating in the water and bobbing up and down with the waves. The gull is not moved along with the wave. Instead, it is first lifted up and moved a bit backward as it rides up the crest of one wave. Then it slides down into the trough and is moved a bit forward. As this action is repeated wave after wave, the gull is moved in a circle, which is the actual motion of the surface water being disturbed by a wave train. The seagull will move forward only if it swims or the wind pushes it.

Now let's return to waves that break onto the beach. The water of a breaking wave moves forward with the wave rather than moving in a circle. If the water were not moving shoreward, a surfer would just bob up and down like a resting gull. But since the surfer is carried shoreward, the water must also be moving him. How? When a wave enters shallow water, it is slowed down and steepens as the circling water beneath it first reaches the bottom and then drags against it. This causes the wave to lose its shape and the water its circular motion. The result is a shoreward plunge of water onto the beach. The steeper the slope of the beach, the higher the waves tend to crest.

The Force of Waves

Waves can be very destructive, as anyone who has witnessed a coastal hurricane knows. A breaking wave crashing against a cliff of limestone or other soft rock wears away the rock in two ways. The sheer physical battering of water against rock breaks down the rock into pebbles and sand. Chemical action of the water also slowly dissolves the rock. Along one coastal section of England, the soft rocks are being washed into the sea by wave action at the rate of 17 feet (5 meters) a year.

Waves commonly carve out sea caves in places where the rock is soft and the waves persistent. Sea caves are found along the shores of oceans and large lakes. They are formed by hundreds or thousands of years of wave action. Over time, the pounding water breaks away weak and loose pieces of rock. Also, sand and gravel carried by the water chip away at the rock like millions of tiny hammers. Eventually a cave is formed and keeps getting larger. The Pacific coast of the United States has many sea caves. One of the most famous is Sea Lion Cave in the state of Oregon.

The most destructive kind of wave is the one called a *tsunami*, popularly known as a "tidal wave" although it has nothing to do with tides. The word comes from the Japanese words for "harbor" and "wave." The people of Japan seem to experience these fierce waves more often than anyone else.

Tsunamis are triggered by undersea earthquakes. When the ocean-floor bedrock snaps up and down, rather than from side to side, along a fault line, huge amounts of energy are transferred to the water and generate these killer waves. At first the tsunami is only a mound of water at the sea surface. At that stage, gravity acts to level the water. The result is a series of three or four broad waves with a wavelength greater than the average 3-mile (4.8-kilometer) depth of the ocean. Since a tsunami's wavelength is very long, the wave travels very fast. Some have been known to speed through the deep ocean at up to 500 miles (805 kilometers) an hour. Despite the speed of such a wave, and the enormous amount of energy it packs, on a ship at sea you don't even notice one passing by. The reason is that the tsunami rarely is more than 1 or 2 feet (.5 or so) high.

The tsunami puts on its grand show only when it begins to sweep into shallow water. As it approaches the land, it begins to drag against the bottom. That causes a rapid decrease in speed to only about 50 miles (80 kilometers) an hour and a rapid buildup in height. The wave crests to a height of 100 feet (30 meters) or more as the water behind the wave quickly piles up. Finally, the tsunami crashes down with terrible destructive force onto any coastal village in the way.

On October 6, 1773, one of the greatest tsunamis on record flooded the coast of Cape Lopatka, on the southern tip of Kamchatka Peninsula in the far east of Russia. By the time the wave reached shore, it towered 210 feet (64 meters) into the air. On June 15, 1896, an undersea earthquake 125 miles (201 kilometers) from the Sanriku district of Japan set up a tsunami that swept in and broke 100 feet (30 meters) high onto the shore. After the waters receded, twenty-seven thousand bodies and debris from more than ten thousand houses lay strewn about or were carried into the sea by the wave's backwash.

One eyewitness to a devastating tsunami wave chain that crashed down onto the island of Hawaii in 1946 described the event in these words:

"The waves of the tsunami swept toward shore with steep fronts and great turbulence. Between crests the water withdrew from shore, exposing reefs, coastal mud flats and harbors' bottoms for distances up to 500 feet [152 meters] or more. The outflow of the water was rapid and turbulent, making a loud hissing, roaring, and rattling noise. At several places houses were carried out to sea, and in some areas even large rocks and blocks of concrete were carried out onto the reefs. People and their belongings also were swept out to sea."

Just as waves sometimes eat away at the land, they can also build new land. Along the Atlantic coast south of New England, as well as the Gulf of Mexico coast, enormous amounts of quartz sand are shaped and reshaped by the restless sea into a variety of attractive landforms. Wide beaches, backed by dunes and separated from the mainland by shallow bays or marshy lagoons, typically define a coast dominated by barrier islands. On such building coasts, long ridges of sand called spits may project many miles from the land. In other places, sandbars may grow and completely cross a bay, disconnecting it from the open ocean.

Ocean Currents

You can walk along just about as fast as an ocean current moves. The surface currents are driven by the wind and so tend to be water's counterparts of the major prevailing-wind systems described in chapter 6. Because the surface currents are wind driven, they do not run much deeper than a few hundred feet.

In spite of their shallowness, the surface currents are very effective movers of heat and cold from one location to another. In far northern and southern latitudes, for three months or more in winter, the air temperature over the water may be well below freezing. If water were not such a good storer of heat, the oceans at these latitudes would cool quickly, freezing to great depths, and could not support as much life as they do.

If water lost heat rapidly, it also would gain heat rapidly. So in summer the ocean's surface waters at and near the Equator would become very hot. Such extreme water temperatures in both winter and summer would bring about major changes in the way living things are distributed throughout the oceans. They would also change the pattern of the major ocean currents and the vital role those currents play in the planet's climate.

One example is what happened to the Gulf Stream current when it changed its course. The Gulf Stream is a "river" of warm water that flows out of the Gulf of Mexico, crosses the Atlantic Ocean south of Newfoundland, and flows toward Europe in a northeasterly direction. As it does, it breaks into two major branches, one flowing northward toward the British Isles and the other looping southward. The northbound current then branches again, one arm flowing toward Iceland. The warm water of the Gulf Stream provides Iceland, Britain, and parts of Scandinavia with a moderate climate.

In the mid-1700s, the Gulf Stream gradually began to shift its transatlantic course from northeast to east, and by about 1780 it was flowing in a slightly southeasterly direction. The effect of this change was to push the warm waters of the Sargasso Sea area of the Atlantic Ocean south, permitting cold Arctic water to move farther south. The result was a southward invasion of drift ice around Iceland, cooler summers, and colder winter winds, a period that came to be known as the "Little Ice Age." It wasn't until well into the 1900s that the Gulf Stream resumed its earlier nearly northeast course.

Two major current systems cause many complex movements of water in most other parts of the world's oceans. They are the great North Equatorial and South Equatorial Currents. The trade winds blowing from the northeast in the Northern Hemisphere and from the southeast in the Southern Hemisphere drive both currents westward across the Atlantic and Pacific Oceans. When the currents strike land, they are deflected. The North Equatorial Current is deflected northward as, for example, the

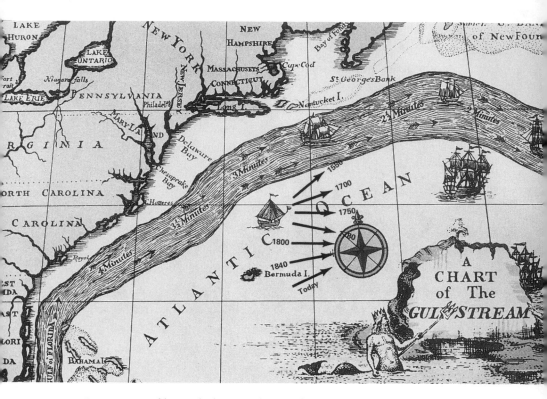

Benjamin Franklin made this map showing the course of the Gulf Stream in 1770. The arrows with dates above them show how the course of the Gulf Stream changed over the years from 1550 to the present.

Gulf Stream in the Atlantic Ocean and the Kuroshio Current in the Pacific Ocean off Japan. In the Southern Hemisphere, the South Equatorial Current is deflected southward as, for example, the Brazil Current off South America's east coast.

Sandwiched between these two major current systems is the Equatorial Countercurrent that flows eastward in the Atlantic, Pacific, and Indian Oceans. Because of complex and variable winds in the Indian Ocean, the current system there is complex. Many lesser currents of cold polar water in the Northern Hemisphere flow southward and mix with the warmer water of the North Equatorial Current. Such lesser currents include the Oyashio Current from the Bering Strait and the Labrador Current from

Smith Sound and Baffin Bay. In the Southern Hemisphere such lesser currents include the cold Humboldt Current, which flows up South America's west coast, and the West Australian Current, which flows out of the Antarctic up Australia's west coast.

In addition to the surface currents are the sluggish and cold deep-water currents. These currents are set up by a combination of events: the planet's rotation, which twists the currents; the Sun's heating of the water in the tropics; and the polar ice cooling the oceans in high latitudes of both hemispheres. Because warm water is lighter than cooler water, the warmer water floats on top. Deep down in the oceans, the water is much colder, in many places only a few degrees above freezing. The cold water flowing from the Arctic and Antarctic toward the Equator tends to sink as it enters regions of warmer water. Where these deep currents come up against the land, they rise to the surface and carry with them mineral nutrients. So in some places the ocean waters are kept well mixed by upwellings. Such upwellings take place along the coasts of California, Chile, and southwest Africa.

Along some coasts, the winds from the land blow over the water. Where this happens, the surface water along the coast is driven away from the shore. The colder water 330 feet (100 meters) or so deep then rises and replaces the water that has been driven away. Rich in nutrients, this cold water is now warmed by the Sun. When that happens, there is a great outburst of growth of plant and animal plankton. Fish are attracted to these rich, watery pastures in large numbers. And so are birds that feed on the fish. So the currents, especially the deep-flowing ones, play a very important part in maintaining the webs of life in the oceans.

The Restless Tides

The most obvious change we can see in the oceans is the coming in and going out of the tides. Many centuries ago, mariners accustomed to the relatively small tides of the Mediterranean Sea were greatly surprised at the high tides they found in the northern ocean. In 55 B.C., Roman emperor Julius Caesar landed his ships on the English coast during a particularly high tide. Imagine his surprise when, on awakening the next morning, he saw all the ships high and dry near the top of the beach. That was his first experience with a 20-foot (6-meter) spring tide.

The ebb and flow of the tides twice each day are caused by the gravitational tug on the planet by the Moon and Sun. As the Moon slowly glides across the sky, its gravitational tug raises a bulge of ocean water beneath it. In fact, there are two high-tide bulges. One is on the side of Earth facing the Moon, and the other is in a straight line through Earth on the opposite side. The cause of the second bulge can be explained by under-

When the Moon is at first- and third-quarter positions, we have neap (relatively low) tides because the Sun and Moon attract the ocean water from slightly different directions. We have spring (relatively high) tides at new moon and full moon. At those times the gravitational pull of the Sun and Moon are aligned and so act together.

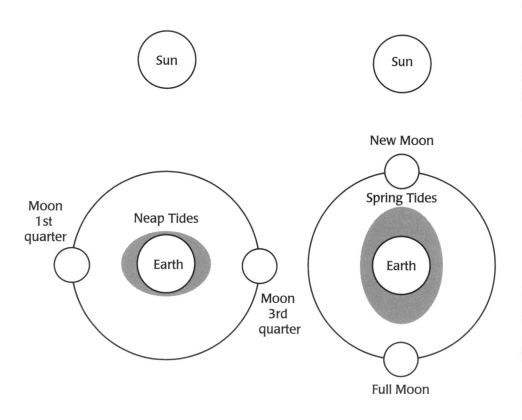

standing that the strength of gravity depends on distance. The closer two planets or other objects are together, the greater the gravitational force attracting them to each other. Increase the distance and you decrease gravitational attraction. The second tidal bulge on the far side of Earth, as shown in the diagram, is caused by the water on the far side being farther away from the Moon than the tidal bulge on the side of Earth facing the Moon. In effect, the second tidal bulge is "left behind" because the Moon's gravity is attracting the surface water less strongly than it is attracting the ocean floor just beneath the bulge.

If Earth spun on its axis at a rate that matched the Moon's passage overhead, the two high tides on opposite sides of the planet would just sit there all the time, as would the two low tides at their opposite positions. But Earth's rotation is such that the planet rotates beneath the two tidal bulges locked in position more or less in line with the Moon. Because Earth takes 24 hours to complete one rotation, New York City, for example, has one high tide at noon, say, then a second high tide 12 hours later. Halfway in between, it also has two low tides.

It turns out that two successive high tides do not occur exactly 12 hours apart, rather every 12 hours and 25 minutes. The "extra" 25 minutes come from the Moon's orbital motion around Earth. During the time Earth is making a full rotation of 24 hours (called the *solar day*), the Moon keeps moving eastward along its orbit. So each full day of 24 hours, Earth must rotate an additional 50 minutes to "catch up" and place the Moon once again directly overhead. That 24-hour-and-50-minute period is called the lunar day. You can measure this "catch-up" time yourself by timing the moment of moonrise over several nights.

Although the Sun is some twenty-seven million times more massive than the Moon, its gravitational tug on the tides is only half as strong because the Sun is so very far away. Nevertheless, the Sun does play a role in Earth's tides. Whenever the Sun, Moon, and Earth are aligned, the Sun's tide-raising ability is added to that of the Moon and we have especially high tides, called *spring tides*. Such alignments take place at full moon and new moon, as shown in the diagram. But when the Moon swings around in its orbit to its first-quarter position and then to its third-quarter position, gravitational attraction of the Sun and Moon act against each other, and we have only small tides, called *neap tides*.

Generally the ocean tides tend to be small, amounting to only a few feet or meters. However, in some places, such as Canada's Bay of Fundy and England's Bristol Channel, the shape of the land produces tides as high as 50 feet (15 meters). The incoming tide rushes up certain of the world's rivers as a *tidal bore*. A bore may be a series of low, rolling waves that travel upstream at only a few miles (kilometers) an hour. Or it may be a raging, foaming wave of destruction. The world's largest tidal bore churns its way up China's mile-wide (1.6 kilometers) Tsientang River as a wall of water 10 feet (3 meters) high that speeds along at about 15 miles (24 kilometers) an hour.

Tidal Friction Lengthens Earth's Day

The tidal friction against the ocean floor acts as a brake that steadily slows Earth's rotation. Measurements over the past three hundred years show that our days are getting longer by 0.002 seconds a century. Although that is not very much over a few decades or centuries, it adds up over the planet's four-billion-year history.

By studying the daily growth rings of the fossils of marine organisms that lived millions of years ago, scientists can read day length through geologic time. Such organisms that lived early in the Cambrian period, about 570 million years ago, reveal a day length of only 21 hours. That means that a Cambrian year must have had 424 21-hour days. Tidal friction has continued to lengthen our days, and shorten our years, with the result that today we have 24-hour days and 365¼ days in a year. This rate of change means that the year loses about one day every 10 million years.

The tides are also causing something even more interesting to happen to the Earth-Moon system. While tidal braking by the Moon is slowing Earth's rotation, the tidal bulge of water facing the Moon is nudging the Moon to gradually spiral outward, away from Earth. The reason is that Earth's rotation beneath the oceans pulls the tidal bulge of water beneath the Moon slightly ahead of a line joining the Moon and Earth, as shown

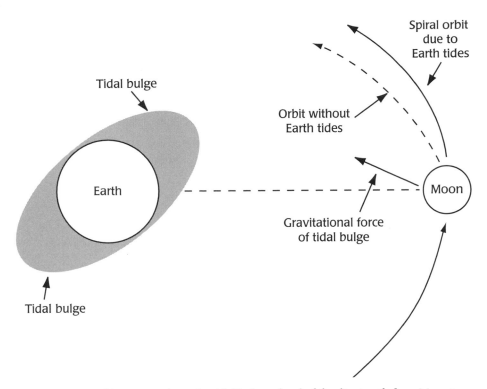

Tidal bulge

Spiral orbit
due to
Earth tides

Orbit without
Earth tides

Earth

Moon

Gravitational force
of tidal bulge

Tidal bulge

Because Earth's rotation drags the tidal bulges ahead of the direct path from Moon to Earth, the mass of the bulges pulls the Moon forward and ever so gradually "whips" it along an outward spiral.

in the diagram. The gravitational tug of this mass of tidal water pulls the Moon forward in its orbit and so causes the orbit to grow larger.

Scientists have measured the Moon's rate of "escape" from Earth by bouncing laser beams off reflectors planted on the lunar surface by the Apollo astronauts. That escape rate is 1.2 inches (3 centimeters) a year, which will increase the Moon's distance from Earth by some 19,000 miles (30,576 kilometers) over the next million years. Somewhere along the way, the slowing down of Earth's rotation will match the Moon's orbital motion. At that distant time, a smaller-appearing Moon will hang motionless in the sky, no longer rising and setting each lunar day.

Nowhere are Earth's oceans more spectacular than as seen from space. In 1990, the *Voyager 1* space probe entered the far reaches of the Solar System and looked back at planet Earth from a distance of 3.7 billion miles (6 billion kilometers). So great was that distance that the electronic snapshot *Voyager* captured took five and a half hours to be sent back to Earth at the speed of light. The picture was a mere point not much larger than the period at the end of this sentence. But the dot was blue. We saw clearly on that February day in 1990 how overwhelming is the blueness of Earth's atmosphere and the oceans that reflect that scattered blue light. Even at that immense distance, the planet continues to display a uniqueness visible nowhere else in the Solar System—a blue planet dominated by the waters of its mighty oceans.

8

Strange World of the Ocean Floor

HMS Challenger

An understanding of the deep seafloor did not begin to unfold until the late 1800s, during the voyage of Her Majesty's Ship *Challenger*. From December 1872 to May 1876, the *Challenger* expedition made the first, and most ambitious, study of the global ocean. Jointly sponsored by England's Royal Society and the British Admiralty, the 68,000-mile (109,432-kilometer) voyage took the ship and its crew of scientists to every ocean except the Arctic.

Throughout the voyage, the scientists sampled the depth of the water by laboriously lowering a weighted line overboard and recording the length of the line let out. In all, they made two hundred fifty deep soundings. During the course of the expedition, 4,417 new species of ocean life were discovered. Information collected from the surface of the sea to its greatest depth revealed for the first time physical features of the seafloor and the chemistry of seawater. Many of the data gathered and published at the time are still in use today. The fifty large volumes form the basis of modern oceanography and marine biology.

As long as ocean depths had to be measured by the use of weighted lines, knowledge of the shape of the seafloor would remain sketchy. Then, in the 1920s, a new technique for "seeing" the ocean floor in much greater detail came into use. The new invention was an electronic depth-sounding device known as the echo sounder.

The instrument works by transmitting sound waves toward the ocean bottom. When the sound waves strike the ocean floor, they bounce back to the surface as an echo. While a delicate receiver records the echo, a clock measures the time interval to fractions of a second. By knowing the speed of the sound waves through seawater—about 4,920 feet (1,500 meters) per second—and the time it takes the energy pulse to reach the ocean floor, scientists can measure the depth from any point on the surface.

Oceanographers studying the topography of the oceans today speak of three major features: the continental margins, the deep-ocean basins, and the mid-ocean ridges. Within each of these units are many individual features.

Continental Margins

In some cases, the continental margins are the edge of a continent as we see it on a world map, such as the West Coast of the United States. In other cases, the true continental margin is hidden beneath the water and extends several hundred miles from shore, such as the East Coast edge of the continent in the United States. So there are two types of continental margins: Atlantic type and Pacific type.

Atlantic-Type Margins An Atlantic-type margin stretches oceanward from the shore as a flat and featureless continental shelf. Some continental shelves extend seaward for only a few miles, whereas others stretch away from the coast 1,000 miles (1,609 kilometers). On average, however, the shelves are about 50 miles (80 kilometers) wide. From the shore to the edge of the shelf, the water deepens ever so gradually. At the seaward edge it usually is about 450 feet (137 meters) deep. The gentle slope of continental shelves is so slight that they appear almost level.

The seaward edge of the continental shelf ends abruptly and dips fairly steeply to the broad ocean floor as the continental slope. You can think of the slope as a ramp angled some 25° directly down to the seafloor, as off the Aleutian Islands near Alaska. Continental slopes mark the boundary between the crustal rock of the continents and the crustal rock of the ocean floor. In some areas, such as the eastern coast of North America, the slope does not lead directly to the deep-ocean floor. Instead it abuts a broad and gently sloping platform called the continental rise. Whereas the width of the continental slope averages about 12 miles (19 kilometers), the continental rise may extend for hundreds of miles onto the deep-ocean basin.

Submarine Canyons Among the most interesting features of the Atlantic-type ocean floor are the many submarine canyons cut deeply into the continental slope. Many of them rival the largest canyons on land and often are 2 miles (3 kilometers) deep. Like the 1-mile-deep (1.6 kilometers) Grand Canyon in northern Arizona, submarine canyons also have towering, V-shaped walls. An interesting thing about their walls is that they are made up of a wide variety of sedimentary, igneous, and metamorphic rock types. They range from soft shales to hard granites and quartzites. Some are geologically very old, others younger. The canyons' rock types clearly show that these features are part of the continents and not members of the rock family that composes the ocean floor.

Like the Grand Canyon, a large submarine canyon may be fed by smaller tributary canyons less deeply cut into the continental slope. All the tributary canyons lead into a main canyon and form a pattern that resembles the veins in a leaf. There can be little doubt that submarine canyons, like their relatives on land, are produced by erosion. The question is, How?

It is along the Atlantic coast, especially from the Hudson Canyon near New York City to the Baltimore Canyon near Maryland, that submarine canyons are best developed. Eight dominate the continental slope in this region. Canyons that are cut into the continental slope are straighter and steeper than those that scar the continental shelf. This suggests that a canyon somehow begins on the slope and then may cut its way backward into the shelf as the slope canyon becomes older and deeper.

As canyons on land are carved out by the flow of river water, the canyons of the continental slopes and shelves seem to be sculpted by the flow of "rivers" of *sediments* that originate on the land. The continental shelf and slope are vast dumping grounds for thick deposits of sediments washed off the land. Rivers carry billions of tons of sediments into the sea every year—particles of rocks, minerals, and soils washed off the continents by seasonal rains and melting snows.

The theory that seems to best explain how submarine canyons are formed involves erosion by powerful sediment slides called *turbidity currents*. A turbidity current is a flow of heavy, sediment-laden, watery slurry that surges violently down the continental slope as fast as 50 miles (80 kilometers) an hour. Its speed down the more gently sloping continental rise slows to about 15 miles (24 kilometers) an hour.

Evidence of the destructive force of a turbidity current first came in 1929. A severe earthquake off the coast of Newfoundland loosened sediments near the edge of the continental shelf and triggered a turbidity current that snapped thirteen transatlantic telephone and telegraph cables. At the time, it was assumed that the tremors from the earthquake had caused the multiple breaks. However, when scientists plotted the locations of the breaks on a map, they noticed that all of them had occurred along the steep continental slope and the gentler continental rise. There were no breaks on the continental shelf.

Since the time of each break was provided by automated telephone records, the pattern of breakage emerged. The breaks high up the continental slope were first, almost at the instant of the earthquake. Breaks farther down the slope came at later intervals, the last occurring 450 miles (724 kilometers) away 13 hours after the earthquake. The farthest breaks obviously had taken place too long after the shock of the earthquake to have been caused by the shock. There could be no doubt that a turbidity current had been almost instantly triggered by the quake and had broken the cables.

After the thick sediment-laden slurry has rushed through the canyon, it spreads out as a feature called a deep-sea fan. The edge of a deep-sea fan usually marks the beginning of the deep-ocean floor, which is a vast and sprawling level region known as the *abyssal plain*. The name comes from the Latin word *abyssus*, which means "bottomless." The abyssal plains are as flat as a parking lot and are among the most level natural features on Earth. The one off the coast of Argentina, for instance, changes

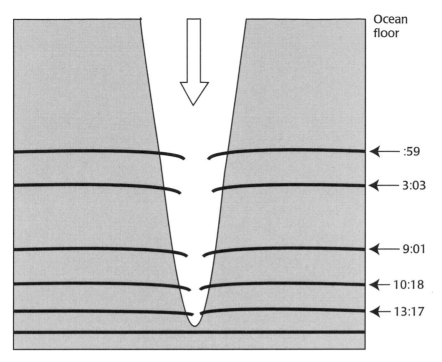

The November 18, 1929, earthquake off Newfoundland touched off a turbidity current that swept down a canyon and snapped a series of transatlantic telegraph cables. From the time intervals between breaks—shown in hours and minutes—scientists could tell that the currents were traveling at about 50 miles (80 kilometers) an hour along the steepest gradients.

less than 10 feet (3 meters) in elevation over a distance of 800 miles (1,287 kilometers). Every ocean on the planet has abyssal plains, which make up almost 30 percent of Earth's surface, nearly equal to the area of all the planet's land area. It is in the Atlantic Ocean where these deep-sea plains are most extensive.

Pacific-Type Margins

If the floor of the Atlantic is regarded as relatively flat and featureless, then the floor of the Pacific Ocean can be regarded as a Disney World of the unexpected. Almost all of the world's deep-ocean trenches are located in the Pacific and plunge to depths of 35,000 feet (10,668 meters) or more.

A section of the Challenger Deep, in the Marianas Trench, is more than 6 miles (10 kilometers) below sea level. Mount Everest could comfortably fit into the trench, with just a bit of its peak poking above the waves. It is the Pacific's trenches that best characterize that ocean's "active" type of continental margin.

Although deep-ocean trenches take up only a small part of the ocean floor, they are one of the most significant landform features. They mark where the leading edge of one crustal plate collides with the edge of another and plunges down into the mantle. The results are earthquake and volcanic activity. Visible examples of such volcanic mountain building are sections of the Andes mountain range in western South America, and the Cascade Mountains of northern California, Oregon, and Washington. Both ranges run parallel to trenches that lie next to continental margins. The melting of a descending plate's leading edge produces the molten rock that wells up.

Deep-ocean trenches are best developed along the edges of the Pacific Ocean, especially its western edge. Landward of the trenches we can expect to find an island archipelago, or chain of volcanic islands. In the case of the Andes and Cascades, the volcanoes lie on the edge of the continent itself; but the islands of Japan, the Mariana Islands, the Philippine Islands, the Aleutian Islands, and the Tonga Islands represent such volcanic island archipelagoes.

During the 1940s, the American seismologist Hugo Benioff discovered something interesting about the relationship between earthquakes and these deep-ocean trenches in the Pacific. Vibrations produced by Earth and vibrations that produce musical sounds both fascinated Benioff. To enable him to "hear" earthquake vibrations, he designed the most sensitive seismograph in use at the time. The instrument could magnify the slightest movement of Earth's crust by about two hundred thousand times. This sensitivity was to be useful in important ways.

In one study of the southwestern Pacific Ocean near the Tonga Trench, for example, Benioff found that earthquake depths increased with distance landward from the trench; that is, the farther from the trench, the deeper the earthquake. Also, earthquakes' points of origin, or foci, follow a pattern

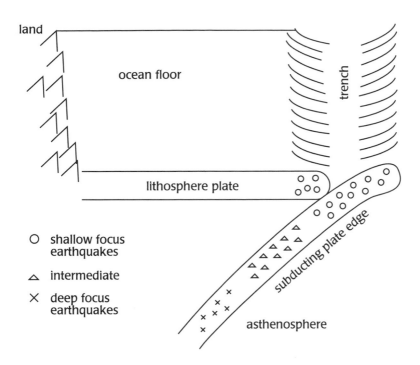

Where one plate "dives" beneath another plate at a subduction zone, earthquake centers are found along that region of the diving plate called the Benioff Zone. The shallowest quakes occur nearest the trench, and the deepest quakes occur progressively farther away from the trench.

of gradually increasing depth down through the ocean floor into the mantle along a slope with an angle of about 45 degrees. These inclined zones of seismic activity came to be called Benioff Zones.

Mid-Ocean Ridges

Vast undersea mountain chains snake their way over the ocean floor for a distance of 43,000 miles (69,100 kilometers). Called mid-ocean ridges, they cover more than 20 percent of Earth's surface and 35 percent of the deep-ocean basin. It is along the crests of these mid-ocean ridges that the rift valleys discussed in chapter 5 occur.

Found in all of the major oceans, mountains making up the undersea ridge system are the single most prominent seafloor feature. Like mountain ranges on a continent, ocean ridges tower above the deep-ocean basins. But there the comparison ends. Continental mountain chains, such as the Alps or Himalayas, are formed mainly of sedimentary rock types that have been crushed and crumpled together like corrugated cardboard. Mid-ocean ridges, on the other hand, are made of enormously thick layers of volcanic rock.

The magma that forms that volcanic rock originates in the asthenosphere and upper mantle. It is then squeezed up through the overlying lithosphere all along the central line of the ridges. It would seem that after the lava hardened into volcanic rock, it would form a plug and prevent more lava from pouring out onto the ridge surface of the lithosphere. What seems to happen instead is that powerful forces within the asthenosphere and upper mantle pull the newly formed volcanic rock of the lithosphere apart, almost like stretching cold taffy. New lava then wells up and fills in the ridge fractures. Meanwhile, the lithosphere on both sides of the ridge slides away from the central line and over the asthenosphere. The process has been going on for many millions of years, the younger lava outpourings pushing aside and replacing the older, hardened volcanic rock. If this new basaltic volcanic rock actually is doing what we think it is doing, then we would expect to find the oldest basaltic rock farthest from the mid-ocean ridge system. That is just what we do find.

The mid-ocean ridge system does not form a smoothly continuous line lacing the globe. Instead, it is broken apart into thousands of fragments, and the fragments are offset from one another like carelessly thrown planks of a walkway. Each fragment is the result of a rupture, or fault, in the rock of the ocean floor. The fracture zones run parallel to the direction of plate movement. The Mendocino Fracture Zone, for instance, is perhaps the best known. It offsets a section of mid-ocean ridge called the East Pacific Rise and enters California as the San Andreas Fault.

Smokers A vast store of magma lies less than a half mile (less than a kilometer) beneath the base of the mid-ocean ridge system. Seawater seeps down through cracks in the ridge's rock, is heated, and is then forced back up to the seafloor through *hydrothermal vents* as hot water that is rich in dissolved minerals. The outpourings of water are called smokers. There are white smokers, and there are black smokers. The white smoker is a cloud of white particles of barium sulfate, a mineral known as barite. The water temperature of white smokers ranges from 86 degrees Fahrenheit (30 degrees Centigrade) to 626 degrees Fahrenheit (330 degrees Centigrade). The black smoker contains various sulfur-bearing minerals that include iron, zinc, lead, and copper. It is those minerals that color the smoker black. The water temperature of black smokers tends to stay right around 662 degrees Fahrenheit (350 degrees Centigrade).

These vents in the seafloor, issuing warm, mineral-rich water, support unusual biological communities. In 1977, oceanographer Robert Ballard first discovered such communities in the Galapagos Mid-Ocean Ridge, located between South America and the Galapagos Islands. He lowered a camera-equipped sled to a depth of 8,000 feet (2,440 meters) to the seafloor. Scientists found it hard to believe what the filming revealed. There were enormous clams, strange crabs, and red tube worms. There also were chimneylike structures as high as 165 feet (50 meters) belching black "smoke." They were powerful undersea geysers. The biological community depends on bacteria that take in hydrogen sulfide gas dissolved in the geyser water from these hydrothermal vents. Both the heat associated with the vents and the rich and varied chemistry of the water provides an excellent energy resource and the necessary nutrients dissolved as chemicals to create food.

It is now thought that the entire volume of ocean water is cycled through this hydrothermal plumbing system over a span of about three million years. The chemical exchange between ocean water and the hot rock below strongly influences the chemistry of the oceans. Oceanographers think that the accumulation of metallic sulfide minerals around the smoker vents is the planet's single most important mineral source for our essential metals.

Long after the rich mineral deposits form in the mid-ocean ridges, they are carried to the continents as the plate of which they are part grinds into a neighboring plate and is forced down into the mantle rock. As the plate rock is melted beneath the continent, it is forced up as magma

Mineral Resources from the Deep-Ocean Floor

The world's hunger for copper, iron, and other economically valuable minerals continues to climb as more and more people are added to the planet's population. Eventually, will we run out of such resources, or will we just have to look in different places? Oil, natural gas, titanium, tin, gold, and diamonds traditionally have been drilled or dug out on the land. Today those minerals are being mined from shallow coastal waters. In the future, the deep-ocean basins may become the major sites of mineral production.

Exploration in the deep-ocean environment has already begun, in a limited way, with the discovery of large deposits of manganese nodules, which are rich deposits of metallic sulfides along mid-ocean ridges. Manganese nodules are rounded, dark lumps of a mixture of minerals. The major mineral is manganese dioxide, which makes up about 30 percent of a typical nodule. Iron, in the form of iron oxide, comes next and makes up about 20 percent of each nodule. Although iron and manganese are important, there are other, more valuable metals included in smaller amounts. Nodules often contain enough copper, nickel, and cobalt to make mining the nodules worthwhile, even though they lie in waters more than 15,000 feet (4,572 meters) deep. Mining operations will become increasingly inviting in the future as world demand for metals increases.

to the surface, carrying its rich mineral store along. We mine such valuable metal-bearing minerals in places like Arizona, Utah, Chile, and on the Mediterranean island of Cyprus. In fact, so much copper occurs on Cyprus that the island was named after the Greek word for copper, *cyprius*.

Between the continental margin and mid-ocean ridge system lies the deep-ocean basin. The size of this vast region—almost 30 percent of

Earth's surface—is roughly equal in area to all the continents. Here we find the abyssal plains, those remarkably flat regions, and steep-sided volcanic peaks called *seamounts*. Although the abyssal plains make up the most level places on Earth, it is the seamounts that are of special interest.

Seamounts Seamounts dot the floor of the Pacific Ocean as isolated volcanic peaks that may rise hundreds of feet above the surrounding ocean landscape. Although these cone-shaped peaks have been discovered in all the world oceans, most are in the Pacific.

Many seamounts begin as volcanoes near the active oceanic ridges. As the volcano continues to build with the outpouring of lava, it eventually breaks through the ocean surface as a glowing and actively erupting island. In the Atlantic Ocean such seamount-islands include the Azores, Ascension, Tristan da Cunha, and Saint Helena.

As time passes and volcanic activity slows, then ceases entirely, a once active seamount-volcano is eroded nearly down to the level of the water. Streams carve ever deeper valleys, until most of the island washes away into the sea. Meanwhile, ocean waves eat away at the shoreline, shrinking the island even more. A million years later, the island's top is gone, and its bulk below the waves has been carried away from the ocean ridge by seafloor spreading.

These flat-topped seamounts were first discovered by geologist Harry H. Hess of Princeton University from soundings that he made in the Pacific Ocean during World War II. He named them *"guyots"* in honor of Arnold Henri Guyot, a Princeton University professor of almost a century earlier.

Coral Reefs and Atolls

Among the most scenic features of the ocean floor are coral reefs and coral atolls. An atoll is a nearly unbroken ring of coral islands enclosing a shallow lagoon. These reefs and atolls are all built of the calcium-carbonate-rich skeletal remains of coral, a sea-dwelling animal.

Coral reefs form mainly in the warm, clear waters of the Pacific and Indian Oceans. Reef-building corals grow best in waters whose average temperature is about 75 degrees Fahrenheit (24 degrees Centigrade). Corals die if there is a sudden temperature change or if they are exposed too long to temperatures below 64 degrees Fahrenheit (18 degrees Centigrade). The reef builders also need bright, sunny water, so they cannot survive at depths greater than about 150 feet (46 meters). With such a narrow range of living conditions, corals are severely limited to where they can grow. Clear and warm water, such as that in the Bahamas, suits these reef builders.

It was the famous naturalist Charles Darwin who first explained how coral atolls form. In 1831 he sailed aboard the British ship HMS *Beagle* on its famous five-year expedition around the world. In trying to understand how atolls are built, he solved a long-standing puzzle. The question was this: How can corals, which require warm, shallow, sunlit water no deeper than about 150 feet (46 meters), build reef structures that reach thousands of feet to the floor of the ocean?

In his classic book *The Voyage of the Beagle*, he wrote: ". . . From the fact of the reef-building corals not living at great depths, it is absolutely

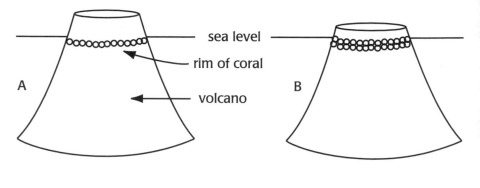

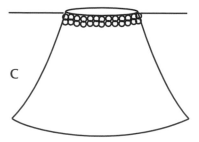

The formation of a coral atoll: At (A) a coral reef forms around the shore of a volcanic island. At (B) the coral grows higher to keep pace with the sinking of the volcano into the seafloor. At (C) an atoll, or rim of coral enclosing a quiet lagoon, has formed as the island's top sinks beneath the waves.

certain that throughout these vast areas, wherever there is now an atoll, a foundation must have originally existed within a depth of from 20 to 30 fathoms from the surface." A fathom is 6 feet (1.8 meters).

Coral reefs, Darwin went on to explain, form on the flanks of sinking volcanic islands. As the ocean floor and its volcanic islands slowly sink, the tips of the islands disappear beneath the water. But as fast as they sink, living corals build up reef complexes that keep pace with the sinking. So there is a continuous new supply of living corals that grow on top of the skeletal remains of the corals that died as the water became too deep and too cold. Darwin said further: "For as mountain after mountain, and island after island, slowly sank beneath the water, fresh bases would be successively afforded for the growth of the corals."

It wasn't until World War II that Darwin's theory of coral-reef formation was proved. In the early 1940s, the United States carried out extensive studies on two Pacific atolls, Eniwetok and Bikini. (At the time, the government was carrying out tests of the newly created atomic bomb.) Drilling thousands of feet into the atolls revealed that volcanic rock did indeed form the base of a coral reef. So atolls, like guyots, owe their existence to the gradual sinking of ocean crust.

Hot Spots and the Hawaiian Islands

More than thirteen hundred years ago, the islands of Hawaii were discovered by Polynesian mariners exploring the vast, uncharted oceans. These daring explorations, perhaps the first ever to venture far out into the ocean world, eventually revealed a planet made up mostly of seas. In present times, the middle of the Pacific Ocean is once again the scene of exploration—modern-day scientific exploration. And the place, once again, is the Hawaiian Islands, for it is there that the new theory of hot spots is unfolding.

Hot spots appear to be plumes of magma welling up from the mantle. They seem to form when a mass of much hotter rock from the core-mantle boundary gradually rises through the mantle. Laboratory experiments suggest that these ascending plumes of magma develop a mushroom-shaped head atop a long, narrow tail. When the hot plume reaches the cooler, lower-pressure region at the base of the lithosphere, the plume flattens and spreads out. The melted rock associated with a plume produces huge amounts of erupting lava at the surface that spreads over a region hundreds of miles across. You can imagine a hot spot as a blowtorch held beneath a plate slowly moving across the flame. So far, more than one hundred such hot spots have been identified. Among them are Iceland in the North Atlantic Ocean, Yellowstone National Park in Wyoming, and the Hawaiian Islands.

Places where geologically ancient hot spots probably operated in the past include continental landforms made up of enormous piles of old lavas. Such "flood basalts," as they are called, include the Columbia River Plateau in Idaho and Washington, the Deccan Plateau in central India, and the Siberian Plateau within the Arctic Circle. When the Deccan Plateau formed about sixty-five million years ago, some 480,000 cubic miles (2 million cubic kilometers) of basaltic lava poured across the land in less than a million years. No present-day volcanic process erupts lava at that incredible rate.

In the Columbia River Plateau, successive flows more than 164 feet (50 meters) thick gradually built up a volcanic plateau of basalt in places almost 2 miles (3 kilometers) thick. Some of the lava stayed molten long enough to spread tens of miles from its source. One such flow spread more than 186 miles (300 kilometers) from its origin and flooded an area of 15,600 square miles (40,000 square kilometers). According to vulcanologist Peter Hooper of Washington State University, "The enormity of this event is hard to visualize. A lava front about 100 feet (30 meters) high, more than 62 miles (100 kilometers) wide, and at a temperature of 2,012 degrees Fahrenheit (1,100 degrees Centigrade) advanced at an average speed of 3 miles (5 kilometers) an hour."

The chain of islands and guyots that extends from Hawaii all the way to the Aleutian Trench has been produced by the movement of the Pacific Plate over one hot spot. As the Pacific Plate slowly glides across the hot spot, one volcanic island after another is popped up out of the sea. The age of each volcanic island serves as a geologic clock that recorded the time when the volcano was perched atop the hot spot.

The oldest of these volcanic islands is a submerged group known as the Emperor Seamount chain that extends southward in a straight line from the eastern tip of the Aleutian Islands. Their basaltic rock is about sixty-five million years old. Extending from these islands is another straight line of mostly submerged volcanoes and guyots called the Hawaiian chain. At the northwestern end of that chain are the Midway Islands. Their volcanic rock is much younger, only about twenty-seven million years old. The next visible island southwest of the Midway Islands is Kauai.

Kauai is the oldest of the large islands that make up the Hawaiian Islands. Its lavas are between four and six million years old. So six million years ago, when Kauai was over the hot spot, it was the only Hawaiian island. As the Pacific Plate kept moving northwestward, away from the hot spot, Kauai became inactive. A new volcanic island, Oahu, formed in its place over the hot spot and the plume that fed it. The lavas of Oahu are between two and three million years old. In its turn, Oahu, too, was moved off the hot spot toward the northwest by continued movement of the Pacific Plate. Next, the island of Molokai formed. Its lavas are between one and two million years old. Then came Maui, whose lavas are even younger, less than one million years old. Today the lava flows of Hawaii, the largest island of the chain, are fed by the ancient, but still very active, hot spot.

As proof of their old age, the volcanic islands of Kauai, Oahu, and Molokai have ancient lavas that have been deeply eroded. There also are no new lavas to feed these old volcanoes. By contrast, the slopes of the island of Hawaii are coated with fresh lava flows. These newly formed lavas have not been around long enough to be deeply eroded. Two of its volcanoes, Mauna Loa and Kilauea, are very active and pour forth enormous amounts of new lava. Those two volcanoes will probably remain active for another half million years or so before they, too, move off the hot spot that feeds them with erupting lava. In fact, a new volcano already is forming to the southeast.

Examination of the ocean floor about 20 miles (32 kilometers) southeast of Hawaii reveals a new volcanic pile, named the Loihi Seamount. Whether Loihi is being fed by the same source as Mauna Loa and Kilauea is a question. But there can be little doubt that in the not-too-distant geological future, another tropical volcanic island will be added to the Hawaiian chain—and the geographic name of this new island is Loiki.

As geologists probe planet Earth from the ground and astronomers study it from satellite observatories, each year brings new information about the present state of the planet and its ancient past. But it now seems that the crystal ball holding secrets about Earth's future may be the seafloor. For it is there that the planet's upper interior is being torn apart along the mid-ocean ridges and is pushed back together again near the deep-ocean trenches. As ocean floors widen, old lithospheric rock is forced down into the upper mantle, melted, and recycled again and again.

9

Earth's Neighbors in Space

To make our study of the planet we call home meaningful, at least in the larger setting of the Solar System, we have two more tasks. One is to see Earth in its uniqueness among its sibling planets. The other is to take its pulse and listen to its breathing to glean some ideas about its health as it endures the most demanding inhabitants among its myriad life-forms—us.

Planets Hot and Cold

We can arrange all matter that makes up the Solar System into four major groups: 1) our local star, the Sun; 2) the inner, terrestrial planets, Mercury, Venus, Earth, and Mars; 3) the outer, gas-giant planets, Jupiter, Saturn, Uranus, and Neptune; and 4) everything else, which includes mysterious little Pluto, a couple billion or so asteroids and meteoroids, and a couple trillion or so comets.

Let's first briefly look at those planets that are so unlike Earth that we can consider them, well, uninteresting. They are certainly interesting as planets, and as cosmic relatives; but because they are relatives so distant from us in our planetary family tree, they bear little resemblance to Earth. Next we will look in some detail at Venus and Mars, relatives that do resemble us and, therefore, interest us very much. The source of our interest lies in the lessons we may learn from them in how best to manage Earth.

Heavily cratered Mercury, as photographed by Mariner 10, is an inhospitable world with only a trace of atmosphere. Frozen in time, the planet appears today as it was several billion years ago. Mercury's closeness to the Sun causes its sunlit surface to heat up to 800 degrees Fahrenheit (427 degrees Centigrade). NASA

Swift little Mercury is the planet closest to the Sun, nearly three times closer than Earth. It is a world with no atmosphere to speak of, without oceans, without rivers. While its sunlit side is heated to 800 degrees Fahrenheit (427 degrees Centigrade), its surface in shadow plunges to −300 degrees Fahrenheit (−183 degrees Centigrade). Like the other planets, and their moons, Mercury has been scarred by thousands of impact craters that formed in its youth when asteroids and comets crashed explosively onto all of the planets and their moons. Because there are no wind or water or other agents of erosion on Mercury, we see the barren, rocky planet almost exactly as it must have been some three billion years or so ago. Mercury is a fascinating world as a planet, but as an object of the Solar System that can teach us very much about our own planetary affairs at home, it holds little interest.

Beyond Mars and the asteroid belt lies the largest planet in the Solar System, Jupiter. It is one and a half times larger than all of the other planets put together and is the first of the four gas giants. We may consider those inhospitable worlds, right along with Mercury, interesting as planets but of little interest in their usefulness to teach us about ourselves.

A composite photograph of Jupiter with its four principal moons. The largest of the four gas-giant planets, Jupiter has a dense atmosphere mostly of hydrogen. Deep down, the atmosphere turns liquid, then to slush, and finally to metallic hydrogen. Jupiter's environment is so different from Earth's that comparison is impossible. NASA

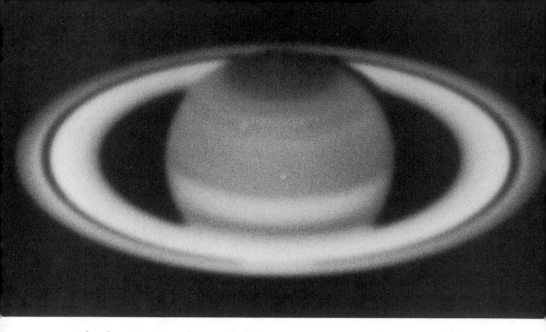

The planet Saturn is the second of the gas giants. In most respects it resembles Jupiter and, therefore, cannot be regarded as a world from which we can learn useful environmental lessons. MOUNT WILSON AND PALOMAR OBSERVATORIES

All four of the gas-giant planets have extremely deep and dense atmospheres. Their gases are mostly hydrogen and helium along with lesser amounts of methane, water vapor, and ammonia. We never see the "surfaces" of these planets, if they can be said to have surfaces, meaning a sharp boundary between a gaseous atmosphere and a solid crust. Instead, their atmospheres just become denser and denser with depth. At and near the top is gaseous hydrogen that turns to liquid hydrogen deeper down and then to hydrogen slush, and finally to metallic hydrogen still deeper. At the planets' centers may be a small molten rock core.

Venus: A Veiled Planet

Venus is very nearly the same size, and has very nearly the same mass, as Earth. And because it was formed at the same time and in essentially the same region of space as Earth, it must also have condensed out of the same kinds of original materials as Earth. So it seems likely that Venus's composition might be rather similar to Earth's in several ways. But there the similarities end, and the question is, Why?

Venus is ever covered by a dense blanket of clouds. The only way we have come to "view" its surface is by landing space probes on the planet and by mapping its surface with radar from satellites put in orbit around it. The surface of Venus is young and may resemble that of Earth several billion years ago when our planet was in the process of forming a solid

Sometimes called Earth's "twin," Venus resembles Earth mainly in size. The planet's extremely dense atmosphere, mostly carbon dioxide, and its effects on Venus's surface interest us most. The atmosphere acts as a giant heat trap that keeps Venus's surface hot enough to melt lead. Increasing our knowledge about Venus's atmosphere can help us better understand the effects of changes we are imposing on our own atmosphere. NASA

crust. The reason for Venus's young surface is massive volcanic activity over the past millions of years, and possibly from the time a crust began to form much longer ago. Although probes have not directly detected volcanic activity on the planet, many lava flows appear fresh. Outpourings of volcanic gases also have been important in determining the nature of Venus's atmosphere.

Where the bulk (78 percent) of Earth's atmosphere is nitrogen, nearly all (96 percent) of Venus's air is the gas carbon dioxide. Only 3.5 percent is nitrogen. The air is so dense that the atmospheric pressure at the surface is nearly a hundred times greater than Earth's surface pressure. Pushing your way through Venus's air while walking around on the planet's surface would almost be like pushing your way through the water as you walked across our deep ocean floor.

Venus's clouds begin at an altitude about 19 miles (30 kilometers) above its surface and extend 37 miles (60 kilometers) skyward. The upper clouds contain traces of carbon monoxide and some water vapor. The carbon monoxide is a result of carbon dioxide molecules being broken down into carbon monoxide and oxygen being given off. The energy that drives this chemical breakdown is ultraviolet radiation from the Sun. For each part of carbon monoxide formed, there should also be one part of oxygen released. In other words, we would expect to find 50 percent carbon monoxide and 50 percent oxygen. But we don't. Instead, there is fifty times less oxygen than that.

Although there are traces of water vapor in Venus's upper atmosphere, the relative humidity seems never to reach even as much as 1 percent, so Earthlike showers cannot occur on Venus. Instead, Venus's clouds are composed of highly corrosive sulfuric acid. In addition, there are hydrogen chloride and hydrogen fluoride. When dissolved in water, those two agents make two other highly corrosive substances: hydrochloric acid and hydrofluoric acid. If any of those substances were in our atmosphere, they would soon combine with the rocky material at the surface and be made harmless. How the acids stay in Venus's atmosphere as clouds is a mystery. The planet's surface must be very different from Earth's.

Russia's *Venera 8* space probe, which landed on Venus in 1972, measured winds aloft blowing at more than 200 miles (322 kilometers) an hour. At the surface, however, the winds were gentle. From an altitude of about 20 miles (32 kilometers) above Venus's surface, a light rain or mist of acid falls through the dense air and eventually to the ground. On Earth, such an acid mist would quickly dissolve sulfur, mercury, lead, tin, and nearly all our surface rocks. Exactly what Venus's surface chemistry is like has yet to be discovered.

Venus's extremely dense and carbon dioxide-laden atmosphere acts as a heat trap for long-wave (heat) radiation from the planet's surface. As a result, there is a *greenhouse effect* that keeps the surface of the planet at a temperature of about 900 degrees Fahrenheit (482 degrees Centigrade), even hotter than Mercury's and hot enough to melt lead, although Venus is farther from the Sun. Earth's large organic molecules of living matter would quickly fall apart in such high temperatures. Venus appears to have the hottest climate in the Solar System, and it can be blamed on the planet's huge store of carbon dioxide, some three hundred thousand times greater than Earth's.

The greenhouse effect, on Venus and Earth alike, works like this. Solar short-wave radiation striking the planet's surface is absorbed by the soil and rocks and oceans. Earth's surface reradiates some of this energy back to the atmosphere as long-wave (heat) radiation. While some of the heat is trapped by carbon dioxide in the air, clouds reflect some of it back to Earth's surface. The same thing happens in a greenhouse. The glass roof permits the entry of short-wave radiation but blocks and traps the exit of long-wave radiation produced by the plants and their soil. In that way, heat builds up in a greenhouse. Perhaps you have noticed that a cloudy winter night usually is less cold than a clear one. The reason is that the cloudless sky lets the long-wave heat energy radiated skyward escape to space.

How can we account for Venus's dense atmosphere of carbon dioxide? Although Earth has about as much carbon dioxide as Venus has, most of ours is locked up in minerals called carbonates. We can imagine a time when Venus more closely resembled Earth in atmospheric density and temperature. But something happened to change its atmosphere, with devastating results to its climate. Possibly the culprit was long-term out-

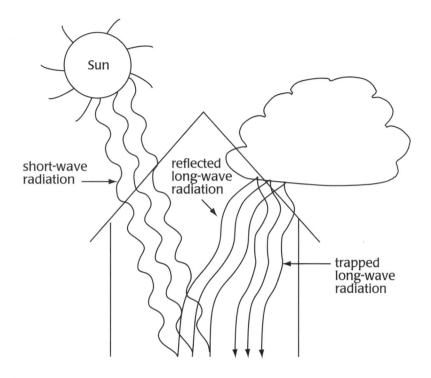

Short-wave radiation striking Earth's surface is absorbed and re-emitted as long-wave (heat) radiation. Clouds reflect this long-wave radiation back to Earth's surface. The same thing occurs in a greenhouse, where the glass roof permits the passage of short-wave radiation but traps the long-wave radiation.

gassing of carbon dioxide by volcanoes, which has continued to the present time. That is why it is important for us to learn as much as we can about the evolution of Venus's atmosphere: By doing so, we will be in a much better position to protect our own.

Because of Venus's closeness to the Sun, we can imagine a greenhouse effect gradually heating up the planet until temperatures at its surface became high enough to boil away all the surface water. Water vapor accumulating in the air would add to the greenhouse effect, trap heat radiated from the surface, and so cause the temperature to soar. Eventually, temperatures would be high enough to liberate the vast stores of carbon dioxide locked up in the rocks.

Here is a second possibility to account for Venus's present state of affairs. Being 30 percent closer to the Sun than Earth is, Venus never cooled enough for water vapor to condense into liquid water. On Earth, oceans formed and absorbed most of the free carbon dioxide in the atmosphere. Much of that carbon dioxide then came out of solution and formed extensive layers of carbonate rocks such as limestone and marble. If that view is correct, then Earth is in little danger of sharing Venus's fate. It's not that Venus got so hot, it's that it never cooled enough to collect water, which would have absorbed all that extra carbon dioxide.

Probably we will never know just what happened on Venus to account for its present inhospitable condition. In the last chapter we will have more to say about possible damaging effects of our pouring more and more carbon dioxide into Earth's atmosphere.

Because Venus and Earth were formed out of the same cosmic soup, we suspect that Venus's interior probably is similar to that of Earth, namely an iron core surrounded by a dense rock mantle. But without seismic soundings of the planet, we cannot be sure.

Mars: The Red Planet

Like Venus, Mars was formed in a region of space neighboring that of Earth, so Mars evolved compounds like those on Earth; for example, minerals made up of varying combinations of magnesium, silicon, iron, oxygen, and sulfur. We know more about the surface and atmosphere of Mars as the result of the Viking missions to Mars in 1976, and more recently the 1997 Pathfinder mission, as described in the following chapter..

Like Earth and Venus, Mars collected its primitive atmosphere long ago by the venting of gases from the hot interior, but this outgassing activity on Mars seems to have been much less than it was on Earth or Venus because Mars is so much smaller, and so it cooled faster. Martian outgassing included carbon dioxide, methane, nitrogen, hydrogen, and water vapor. The planet's low surface gravity (only four-tenths that of Earth's) allowed most of Mars's vented hydrogen to escape. Gradually, the atmosphere

In 1978 the Viking mission to Mars landed on the planet and took this photograph of a rock-strewn surface. Mars rocks are similar to those on Earth. The planet's atmosphere, however, is very "thin" and mostly carbon dioxide. It now seems that Mars might have been somewhat Earthlike in its ancient past. For scale, the large rock at center is about 2 feet (0.6 meters) long. JET PROPULSION LABORATORY

acquired more and more carbon dioxide, which tended to escape less actively because of its heaviness.

Today the Martian atmosphere is 95 percent carbon dioxide, with about 3 percent nitrogen and traces of oxygen and water vapor. Earth has 0.03 percent carbon dioxide. The original amount of nitrogen in the Martian atmosphere probably was ten times the present amount. Nearly all of Mars's water supply is locked up in the planet's polar ice caps and permafrost (compared with 2 to 3 percent for Earth).

If the Martian ice could be released as liquid water, there probably would be enough to form a planetwide layer nearly 45 feet (14 meters) deep. So there is not necessarily a "shortage" of water on Mars. The water just happens not to be available in a liquid state during this particular period in Mars's evolution as a planet. We can regard the planet as gripped in an ice age. Martian winters have blizzards of frozen carbon dioxide snow that rage over one pole. Even on a "warm" summer day the temperature never gets high enough to melt ice. The Martian atmosphere also contains trace amounts of ozone and hydrogen. Quite likely, along with the escape of free hydrogen from the top of Mars's atmosphere, oxygen, nitrogen, and carbon dioxide also are presently escaping.

The Martian atmospheric pressure at the surface is so low that a container of water placed on the surface would vaporize explosively. At one time in the planet's past, the atmosphere may have been about half that at sea level on Earth. The first Mars explorers will have to wear pressure suits, as did the Apollo astronauts who landed on the Moon.

The amount of carbon dioxide in the Martian atmosphere varies from day to night and from season to season; the temperature also varies greatly from day to night and from the Equator to the polar regions. At high noon on the Equator, the temperature goes little above the freezing point. That is because Mars's thin air cannot hold much heat and because of the planet's distance from the Sun. Its average temperature is about −76 degrees Fahrenheit (−54 degrees Centigrade). Since carbon dioxide condenses at such a low temperature, clouds composed of a mixture of traces of water ice, carbon dioxide ice, and dust are common.

When the polar temperatures increase during seasonal change, large amounts of water ice and carbon dioxide ice are vaporized and so temporarily increase the mass of the atmosphere. The denser atmosphere at those times is a better medium to hold heat. That further warms the polar ice and so releases still more carbon dioxide and water vapor. This condition may temporarily build up the Martian atmosphere to densities approaching Earth values.

It now seems that a planet's atmosphere comes from outgassing of the planet during its youth, which in turn depends on the planet's mass and size. Accordingly, small Mercury has virtually no atmosphere, somewhat larger Mars has more atmosphere, still larger Venus and Earth have substantial atmospheres, and the gas-giant planets are mostly atmosphere. But they are mostly atmosphere with a difference. The gas giants' atmospheres did not form from outgassing, but were collected from the original solar nebula of gases and planetesimals.

Has the Martian climate always been as it is today? We can be certain that it has not. Evidence we can read in the surface features of the "Red Planet" point to a time when Mars may have had a climate not too unlike that on Earth today. The Viking missions photographed dead volcanoes and miles of dried-up river beds and vast canyons scoured out by those rivers, proof that long ago, Mars was an active planet.

Like Earth, Mars has a precessional wobble. Whereas it takes Earth about 25,800 years to complete one precessional loop, it takes Mars about twice that long. The late astronomer Carl Sagan once suggested that Mars may now be in the grips of precessional winter, with an extensive polar ice cap in the Northern Hemisphere containing the bulk of the planet's potential atmospheric mass. If so, then 25,000 years ago the planet would also have been in the grip of precessional winter, but that time with the bulk of the atmosphere locked up in the Southern Hemisphere ice cap. But 12,000 years ago, the planet would have been enjoying precessional spring and summer, "a time on Mars of balmy temperatures, soft nights, and the trickle of liquid water down innumerable streams and rivulets,

Old volcanoes are among Mars's geologic features. The largest is Olympus Mons. It is three times higher than Mount Everest. There also are old riverbeds, deep canyons that dwarf the Grand Canyon, and countless craters from past ages. NASA

rushing out to join mightily gushing rivers," according to Sagan. "If so," he goes on, "twelve thousand years ago was a good time on Mars for life similar to the terrestrial sort. If I were an organism on Mars, I might gear my activities to the precessional summers and close up shop in the precessional winters—as many organisms do on Earth for our much shorter annual winters. I would make spores; I would make vegetative forms; I would go into cryptobiotic repose; I would hibernate until the long winter had subsided."

We have taken this detailed look at the atmospheres of Venus and Mars because there are lessons for us Earth dwellers—two that we can do nothing about, but one that may well be within our control. The ones that we can do nothing about are: 1) too much atmosphere, as on Venus, is a bad thing; 2) too little atmosphere, as on Mars, also is a bad thing. The third lesson that we may be in a position to do something about involves control of the amount of carbon dioxide we release into our atmosphere.

To what extent can we keep pouring carbon dioxide and other *greenhouse gases* into our air without running a risk of nudging atmospheric conditions enough to influence a profound change in our climate? That question is much debated these days, and no one knows the answers. One thing does seem certain, however. As the human population continues to grow faster than it ever has in history, we are asking more and more of planet Earth to accommodate our numbers. As our demands on the planet's natural resources grow, so do the amounts of poisonous waste products that we pump into the atmosphere, into the rivers and oceans, and into the ground. It is now time to turn to the second task mentioned at the beginning of this chapter—to examine the health of Earth as a planet under stress.

10

Pathfinder Explores Mars

On July 4, 1997, the United States robot explorer *Pathfinder* landed on the surface of Mars. Its touchdown was cushioned by inflated air bags as the craft bounced along some eighteen times before coming to rest on the rock-strewn field of a region named Ares Vallis. *Pathfinder*, renamed the *Carl Sagan Memorial Station* in honor of the late famous astronomer, became the second successful United States exploration of the Red Planet's battered and rusted surface. The first were the two *Viking* missions to the Red Planet in 1976, which also included a landing on Mars.

On command from Earth's computers, *Pathfinder* opened like a flower. A camera then sent back the mission's first images of nearby rocks and distant hills. It also released a six-wheeled, 23-pound (10.5-kilogram) vehicle about the size of a microwave oven. Named *Sojourner*, the little mobile geologist rolled down a ramp to begin its mission of photographing and prospecting the Martian soil and rocks. In all, *Pathfinder* and *Sojourner* sent back 16,550 photographs of the Red Planet's surface during the four months before their radios went silent, probably because of the extreme Martian cold.

Mars Rocks and Torrential Floods

Pathfinder provided still more evidence of what planetary geologists have long suspected. In times past, the Martian surface was sculpted by raging flood waters and outpourings from volcanoes larger than Ohio and many other states. A landscape littered with rocks and boulders, deep canyons,

Stretching off to the horizon, Mar's surface is a vast stretch of rocks and sand, as viewed in this panoramic sweep taken by the Pathfinder mission to the Red Planet in 1997. There are also enormous ancient volcanoes, now dead. NASA

and aging volcanic hulks is evidence of this. When the robot explorer *Mariner 9* orbited Mars in 1971, it discovered canyons deeper and wider than the Grand Canyon. One, Valles Marineris, measured about 3.5 miles (six kilometers) deep, a hundred miles (160 kilometers) wide, and extended almost 3,100 miles (five thousand kilometers) along the Martian equator. That is the distance between New York City and San Francisco. By comparison, the Grand Canyon is a mile (almost two kilometers) deep, about thirteen miles (twenty-one kilometers) wide, and 217 miles (350 kilometers) long. *Mariner 9* also discovered several huge volcanoes. The largest, Mons Olympus, covers an area the size of Ohio and rises to a height of fourteen miles (twenty three kilometers), twice as high as Mount Everest, Earth's highest mountain.

As *Sojourner* climbed over and bumped into Mars rocks during its exploration, it found and identified one as andesite. Andesite is a volcanic rock rich in quartz and named after South America's Andes Mountains, where the rock type is common. The discovery of andesite on Mars surprised geologists. It told them something about the Red Planet they had not suspected before; that at a much earlier time in the geologic history of Mars, old solidified magmas and lavas had a chance to melt again and again. Such melting and remelting also happens here on Earth. When it does, quartz forms. The presence of quartz distinguishes igneous rocks such as andesite and granite from other igneous rocks that do not contain quartz. Basalt is an example of a quartz-free igneous rock. As it develops, its lava fails to undergo the same process of remelting. Chapters Three and Four describe the way igneous rocks form on Earth.

The discovery of andesite on Mars tells us that early in the Red Planet's life, Mars underwent a geologic history similar to that of Earth. Mars could be much more like Earth than anyone ever thought. Its magmas and lavas separated into both lighter, quartz-rich layers and denser, heavier quartz-free layers. In fact, three months after arriving on Mars and before its radio stopped transmitting, on September 27, *Pathfinder* provided the strongest evidence yet that, like Earth, Mars has a crust, a mantle, and an iron core.

Evidence that the planet is not just a solid ball of rock came from measuring changes in *Pathfinder*'s radio signals as Mars spun on its axis. By comparing *Pathfinder*'s signal changes with changes measured by the earlier *Viking* lander, scientists were given a clue about what the interior of Mars might be like. And more recently the *Global Surveyor* probe, launched after *Pathfinder*, has provided still more clues about Mars's interior.

As we learned in Chapter Four, Earth has an outer molten core of iron-nickel surrounding an inner solid core also of iron-nickel. The planet's magnetic field is produced by the dynamo movement of the outer liquid core. Mars has what we can call a "fossil magnetic field," rather, eight broad magnetic patches within the Martian crustal rock. All of these local fields point in different directions, as if each formed at different times in the Red Planet's history, and as its original global magnetic field grew weaker and weaker. Eventually, the dynamo effect of the liquid core was lost as the core cooled and finally froze solid. Future missions to Mars should cast more light on Mars's deep interior.

Rock samples are scheduled to be brought back from Mars in 2005 to help confirm *Sojourner*'s findings. Meanwhile, additional rover missions are planned for 2001 and 2003. Why all this effort to explore Mars and collect samples of its rocks and soil? Magmas and lavas on both Mars and Earth have similar histories, but only on Earth does the quartz-forming process continue to this day. On Mars it stopped billions of years ago. Why? We don't know. The more we learn about Mars the better we come to understand how Earth developed early in its history. So we study Mars to find out more about our planet.

As *Sojourner*'s metal-treaded wheels churned their way over the boulder- strewn Martian surface and sent information home to us, we had still more questions about the Red Planet. The Ares Vallis region was clearly shaped by flood water of enormous range billions of years ago. The flood left behind a field of rocks and boulders as far as *Pathfinder*'s eye could see. Perhaps release of volcanic heat long ago melted ice trapped underground. The meltwater then gushed over the surface and flowed as broad, swift rivers. The fast-moving water tumbled rocks and sand along, carving out the gullies and terraces we see today. Later, strong winds blew the sand about in gigantic dust storms that still occur.

But what happened to all the water? None remains today, although huge amounts are locked up as ice in the planet's northern polar cap. More may lie frozen as permafrost below the surface.

One of the strongest additional pieces of evidence that Mars was once a lot like Earth is the presence of pebbles. Planetary geologists think the pebbles came from conglomerate rocks. Conglomerates on Earth are a mix of rock types ranging in size from small pebbles to larger gravel, something like peanut brittle. The pebbles and gravel pieces are distinctly rounded, like the peanuts within the matrix of brittle. Since conglomerate rock is sedimentary, it forms in the presence of water. The rounded shapes indicate that the original sharp edges and corners were ground smooth naturally as they were tumbled along by the flowing water.

Life on Mars?

The question on most everyone's mind: Did life ever begin in ancient Martian waters? Early in their histories both Earth and Mars had vast amounts of water, dense atmospheres, and climates warmer than on Earth today. But the Martian surface is not the life-friendly place it once was. *Pathfinder* found daily temperatures on Mars ranging from 32 degrees Fahrenheit to -148 degrees Fahrenheit (0 degrees Centigrade to -100 degrees Centigrade), temperatures so low that carbon dioxide freezes. The highest noon temperature was only -8 degrees Fahrenheit. Wind gusts quickly dropped the temperature by another thirty degrees or more. Winds up to 170 miles an hour (270 kilometers) raged for weeks. Even though the atmosphere of Mars is very thin—only one percent as dense as that on Earth—there are extensive dust storms that sandblast the surface rocks and

The robot geologist explorer Sojourner *bumped and ground its way along as it photographed and prospected the Martian soil and rocks. Together,* Sojourner *and* Pathfinder *sent back to Earth a treasure chest of 16,550 photographs.* NASA

scour out valleys. The dust storms seem to be responsible for the spectacular color changes observed by *Pathfinder*. The images radioed to Earth by both *Viking* and *Pathfinder* show a Martian landscape almost identical to Earth's rocky deserts, complete with sand dunes. *Pathfinder* showed unquestionably the first signs of true sand, with grains ranging from the size and texture of fine beach sand to the fineness and softness of flour.

Our unsuccessful attempt at finding any traces of Martian life on the planet's surface may be because we are looking in the wrong place. Some biologists think we should be looking deep beneath the soil, possibly thousands of feet down. So the question is not about life *on* Mars, but life *in* Mars. In Chapter Seven we described one of the more recently discovered features on Earth's ocean floor. These were the "smokers," undersea geysers, where the water chemistry and high temperatures would seem to prohibit life from occurring. Instead, life abounds, life so strange that it is impossible to imagine such living forms on Earth. These organisms do not eat as we do. They lack mouths and a digestive system. Their "food" comes from special bacteria that live inside their bodies. The nutrients produced by these bacteria go directly into the tissues of the animals. Science fiction could not have imagined a stranger life-form, and right here on Earth, and in such an inhospitable place. Now let's look at another seemingly unusual situation here on Earth—life deep underground.

We have found rich concentrations of liquid hydrocarbons tens of thousands of feet below the ground in the Middle East, the Gulf of Mexico, West Texas, the Black Sea region, the North Sea, Indonesia, and other parts of the world. Hydrocarbons are molecules made of hydrogen and carbon atoms. Crude oil, or petroleum, is made up of hydrocarbons. We drill deep wells to remove these liquid hydrocarbons and convert them into thousands of products, including gasoline and motor oil. Bacteria probably exist at these great depths and are involved in the formation of petroleum (from the two Latin words *petra* ["rock"] and *oleum* ["oil"]). These kinds of molecules were recently found in a Martian meteorite discovered in Antarctica.

Where do these hydrocarbon molecules come from? Not only are they common on Earth, and seemingly so on Mars, but they are also widespread throughout our Solar System and Milky Way galaxy. They are plentiful in the atmosphere of Saturn's large satellite, Titan. Many asteroids have chemical characteristics that match hydrocarbons. Even captured interplanetary dust grains have hydrocarbon compounds. They seem to be everywhere.

Hydrocarbon molecules can form on a planet if carbon and hydrogen combine under high pressure and high temperature. Just such conditions are found thousands of feet underground. Yet-to-be-discovered microscopic life may also be found at those great depths within Earth and within Mars. Such microbes may be the source of the hydrocarbon molecules making up those vast underground seas of petroleum known to form at depths greater than sixty-three miles (one hundred kilometers). The microbes could survive and flourish if there is a supply of carbon and a source of chemical energy "food." Hydrocarbons are a possible source of that food, but only in the presence of oxygen. The oxygen could come from such oxygen-bearing compounds as iron oxides and sulfur oxides.

Until the arrival of *Mars Global Surveyor* in September 1997, the Red Planet had not been under such close examination for nearly twenty years. This is a new beginning for the National Aeronautical and Space Administration (NASA) toward understanding our important planetary neighbor. Many questions remain, but as each is answered, we come to know better the events that shaped the history of Mars—and the history of our own planet. Today Mars is a dead place while Earth continues as a lush world abundant with water and diverse animal and plant life. Could Earth meet a fate similar to that of Mars? And if so, would it be by the hands of its human inhabitants, or would it be by natural forces beyond their ability to control?

11

A Planet Under Stress

So far in this book we have examined Earth's formation as a planet some 4.6 billion years ago. We have sampled its environmental changes through geologic time and ridden its continents as they drift about on giant stone plates. We have examined the forces generated deep beneath the crustal rock that are thought to drive plate movement. We also have probed into the planet's deep interior and climbed up through its atmosphere to the edge of space. And we have traveled its oceans and surveyed its seafloor.

It is now time to examine our planet in midlife, to check its health while it is under the managed care of the only species consciously capable of altering it for good or bad. According to William S. Fyfe of Canada's University of Ontario, "As human population grows by almost ninety million a year, and moves toward ten billion in the new century, humanity's influences will have an even more profound effect. Only recently have we really become aware of what we are doing—you cannot hide from a satellite!"

First we will consider Earth's short-term future, which its human inhabitants are affecting more than we realize or, in some cases, care to admit. Then we will try to read its long-term future as a planet, a future orchestrated by chance events of the cosmos.

Earth's Short-Term Future

Climatologists look for trends as possible pointers to climate change over the next few centuries. A buildup of greenhouse gases in the atmosphere

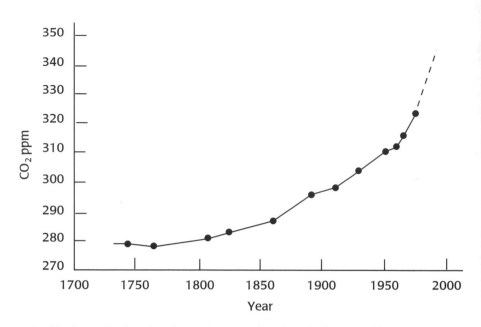

World release of carbon dioxide into the atmosphere from the burning of fossil fuels from 1750 to 1980. Carbon dioxide levels are determined by analyzing the air trapped as bubbles in ice cores from Antarctica.

is one such trend that has been noticeable for well over a century. The hottest four years of any decade since 1900 occurred during the 1980s. Some scientists say that the drought that gripped the United States in 1988 probably marked the beginning of a warming trend due to the buildup of carbon dioxide and other greenhouse gases. On the basis of the present warming trend, NASA climatologist James Hansen has said that he is 99 percent certain that the greenhouse effect has started. "It has been detected and is changing our climate now," he told a U.S. Senate committee hearing as early as June 1988. The biggest offender in releasing carbon dioxide into the air is the United States, which emits some 1,394 million tons a year, or about 23 percent of the world's total. The second-worst offender is China, which emits 807 million tons each year.

Global warming—if, in fact, that is the direction we are headed—will have different effects in different parts of the world. Shifting wind patterns might increase rainfall over parts of Africa that are presently relatively dry. Growing seasons might be lengthened in parts of the former Soviet Union, Canada, and Scandinavia. The United States might be less lucky; with 40 percent less rainfall than it gets now, its wheat and corn belts would dry up. Water tables in such regions would lower, and the water supplies for regions along the coasts would become useless as they were invaded by salt water.

Can anything be done to slow the buildup of greenhouse gases? Today we are adding to the atmosphere's carbon dioxide reservoir at the rate of 4 percent a year. Carbon dioxide levels in the atmosphere are higher now than they have been for one hundred fifty thousand years. Many experts say that we must try to slow that 4 percent rate. If we could slow it to 2 percent a year, the big heat might not come until the year 2050. That delay could give us time to breed new crops capable of tolerating heat and drought, redesign and rebuild selected port cities, and relocate endangered coastal populations inland—all in preparation for a significant rise in sea level as the melting of the polar ice caps speeded up. At this stage of our limited knowledge, about the only thing that seems certain is that we have recently entered a new era of short-term planetary warming.

Let's take a closer look at what seems reasonably certain about sea-level change due to short-term planetary warming. As Earth warms over the next century, sea level can be expected to rise anywhere from 3 to 10 feet (1 to 3 meters). This will be due partly to the expansion of the warming water itself. Warmer water occupies a greater volume than colder water does. Sea-level rise will be due also to the increased melting of glacial ice. The results of such rising, and flooding, could be devastating, especially if at the same time a coastline happened also to be sinking due to crustal movement. Today about 44 percent of the United States population lives within two hours of the coast, and the percentage is increasing.

Along flat coastal areas where the seafloor slope is only a foot (30 centimeters) or less per mile, a rise in sea level of only 1 inch (2.5 centimeters) could cause the sea to move inland some 300 feet (91 meters). Even though rising sea level is a gradual event, we feel it in our lifetimes. When hundreds

If global warming leads to the melting of the ice caps, sea level would rise nearly 300 feet (483 meters). Coastal cities such as New York, Tokyo, and London would be under water. The southern tip of New York's Manhattan is shown here.

of houses are lost to the sea during a powerful storm, property owners simply blame beach loss and property loss on the storm. What they fail to realize is that the next storm of equal force will bring even greater destruction, due to the much greater land area that is susceptible to damage.

Tide measurements made at New York City, where the shoreline is relatively stable, show a sea-level rise of almost 10 inches (25 centimeters) between the years 1900 and 1970. If that trend continues, plan to take a boat to the Statue of Liberty's hemline and say goodbye to Long Island and Miami Beach.

If the addition to the atmosphere of one gas (carbon dioxide) can cause problems, so can the removal of another gas: ozone. Every time an old refrigerator or air conditioner is crushed for junk, a substance known as Freon is released into the air. Freon contains the gas chlorine. Also, as the giant supersonic passenger planes cruise through the stratosphere, they release large amounts of the chemical nitric oxide.

Both chlorine and nitric oxide find their way into the layer of gases in the stratosphere called the ozone layer. Ozone is a form of oxygen that has three atoms instead of two.

The ozone layer is a thin, vital veil that protects us from the high-energy ultraviolet radiation from the Sun. With a thinning of the ozone layer, humans run a higher risk of contracting skin cancer, eye disease (cataracts), and damaged immune systems. Yields of agricultural crops decrease, touching off famines. Larval forms of some marine life are destroyed, upsetting a basic link in the oceanic food chain. And a slight warming of the atmosphere takes place.

Warnings about damage to the ozone layer were first sounded in 1974, but some scientists doubted that the situation was serious. Then, in 1985, a leak in the ozone layer over Antarctica was discovered. It was a gaping hole as large as the United States. We now know that there would be no ozone hole without that class of chemicals known as CFCs (chlorofluoro-carbons). Those compounds are used in the manufacture of refrigerants, cleaning fluids, spray-can propellant, and plastic foam, to name only a few..

In 1991, the Environmental Protection Agency (EPA) announced that the ozone problem is far worse than anyone had thought. The United States has lost 4 to 5 percent of its ozone layer since 1978. Sweden has lost 8 percent. According to an EPA estimate, ozone-layer loss over the United States alone can be expected to cause two hundred thousand deaths from skin cancer during the next fifty years. The EPA warned that if nations did not agree to reduce the use of CFCs, an estimated three million people either alive today or born before 2057 could be killed by exposure to ultra-violet radiation.

The two most common ozone-killing agents are the chlorofluoro-carbon $CFCl3$ and Freon. Once they enter the atmosphere, they have an active life of ozone destruction that lasts from 64 years for $CFCl3$ to 108 years for Freon. When the gases reach high altitudes, they are broken down by ultraviolet radiation and release their chlorine. The released chlorine then attacks ozone molecules.

Alarmed by the destruction of the ozone layer, twenty-four nations agreed in 1987 to cut their production of CFCs in half by the year 2000. China and India refused to cut their use of the chemicals. But because of the long life of ozone-destroying chemicals already in the atmosphere, and the amounts that will be added over the next twenty years or so, reversing the problem—if it can be reversed—will take time. During that time, human life will continue to be put at risk. If nations of the world continue to ban CFCs, the ozone layer could begin to heal sometime around the year 2000. Then it would take about another fifty years for full recovery. However, if some countries decide to renew their use of CFCs, destruction of the ozone layer will be irreversible.

Carbon dioxide and CFCs are only two agents of pollution that pose significant threats to the health of the planet's environment. There are many others, such as nitrous oxide, another ozone destroyer. It is produced by the use of nitrogen fertilizers, which is expected to increase by hundreds of percent in our short-term future in order to help feed the mushrooming human population.

Earth's Long-Term Future

Earth's ultimate fate as a planet does not depend on the behavior of one or more of its species. That has been shown time and again in the planet's long biological history. For more than a billion years, species have come and gone as climates have changed and as the planet has been battered and dented by asteroid and comet impacts. Many scientists now agree that one such asteroid bomb caused, or at least contributed to, the death of the dinosaurs some sixty-five million years ago. Just as there were countless such catastrophic collisions with cosmic objects long before the dinosaurs came into their own more than two hundred million years ago, there will be many more in Earth's long-term future.

The ultimate fate of Earth, however, lies not in calamitous events— natural or manmade—here at home. In the course of evolutionary history, wholesale extinctions of millions of species have only opened new evolutionary opportunities for other species to thrive and flourish, sometimes on even grander scales. No, the shaper of the planet's ultimate fate lies elsewhere, far beyond its frail atmosphere and seas. It is Earth's principal provider and sustainer of life, the Sun, that will shape our long-term future. And we will have nothing to say about it.

Like all stars, the Sun must one day go out and stop powering Earth's three principal life-support systems—global circulation of the atmosphere, the planet's vast store of liquid water, and its cover of green plants, which are the basic energy source for virtually all organisms. It has been only since the 1960s or so that astronomers have come to learn enough about the internal workings of Sunlike stars to predict their demise. Among those astronomers are I.-Juliana Sackmann, of the California Institute of Technology in Pasadena, and her colleagues.

In the first chapter we left the Sun as a fully formed star shining as we see it shining today. The Sun is an immense globe of mostly hydrogen, so large that one hundred Earths could be strung across its diameter and a million Earths would fit inside. The extremely high pressure and temperature created in the core region of such a massive object gradually fuse the lightest of all elements, hydrogen, into the second-lightest element, helium. With each fusion reaction, a small amount of hydrogen mass is converted into a relatively large amount of energy. It is that relationship between small mass loss and great energy production that enables the Sun to shine for billions of years. The energy works its way up through the Sun, bursts out of its surface, and crosses the 93 million miles (150 million kilometers) of space to Earth in just under 8 minutes. We see and feel that energy as light and heat. And as you found earlier in this chapter, there is damaging energy as well, in the form of destructive ultraviolet radiation that is blocked by the ozone layer in the upper atmosphere.

So the Sun's fuel for energy production is its core hydrogen. The question we must face is what happens when the core hydrogen fuel has been used up and no more is available for fusion reactions. Astronomers know enough about the Sun to say that it has enough core hydrogen to shine as we see it today for a total life span of about ten billion years. They know also that the Sun's nuclear fires have been burning for some five billion years, which means that the Sun has another five billion years as a more or less steady-state star. But what happens after that?

In any star that shines more or less steadily, as the Sun does, a constant tug-of-war rages between gravity and pressure. Gravity causes the entire mass of the star to try to tumble into the core region. Meanwhile, pressure within the core, generated by high temperature, pushes outward just enough to balance the gravitational infall of the star's upper layers. As long as nobody wins the tug-of-war, all is well, and the star shines more or less steadily.

In the short run, pressure sometimes wins, and gravity also sometimes wins. But these are brief bouts as measured by cosmic time. A star's nuclear furnace sometimes burns hot for a while, then it may burn somewhat cooler for a while. During these stages of uneven burning, the star balloons out and then shrinks, brightens and then fades, for a while. These periods of brightening and fading interest climatologists as well as astronomers, as you found in chapter 6.

On the whole, however, the Sun seems to have been ever so slowly brightening over its lifetime, and astronomers expect its brightening to continue. In its youth the Sun probably was some 30 percent dimmer than it is today. A little more than a billion years from now astronomers believe it will have become some 10 percent brighter than it is today.

Ten percent may not sound like much, but the resulting increase in energy output will be devastating for life on Earth, according to James F. Kasting of Pennsylvania State University. Kasting expects the brightening to trigger a runaway greenhouse effect on Earth. If intelligent beings still inhabit the planet by that time, they most likely will be helpless to prevent it. Gradually the oceans will heat to the boiling point and vaporize. Life as we know it will no longer be possible. Although that time will mark the end of life on the planet, it will not mark the planet's end. Possibly Earth will have developed a Venuslike atmosphere, beneath which forces within the planet will continue to reshape its unbearably hot surface.

Now let's move the geological clock ahead: It is 6.5 billion years from now. The Sun's nuclear furnace burns not another 10 percent hotter, but more than 200 percent hotter. By now all of the core hydrogen has been used up and replaced by helium. Although the core is not yet hot enough to fuse helium, it is hot enough to begin burning the shell of hydrogen just outside the core.

This new fuel source gives the Sun a temporary burst of energy. Pressure wins a tug-of-war with gravity and puffs up the Sun's outer gas layers, causing it to swell into a giant star. As the outer gases expand, they lose heat and so shine with a cooler red light instead of their hotter yellow light of earlier times. Over some 1.3 billion years, the Sun has become a star that astronomers call a *red giant*. During that time, it has ballooned out to about 166 times its present size, and its nuclear furnace is pouring out 2,300 times more energy than before. If there were still life on Earth, it would be burned to a crisp.

During its period of red gianthood, some eight billion years from now, the Sun is so large that it swallows up and vaporizes Mercury. Its outer, burning gas layers extend beyond the present orbit of Venus, three-quarters of the way to Earth's orbit. On its way to red gianthood, it casts off huge amounts of its gaseous mass, possibly as much as a quarter of it. With less mass than before, the Sun's gravitational pull on Earth weakens. The rule in the cosmos is that the more mass an object has, the stronger its gravitational attraction. With a weakened gravitational grip acting on it, Earth and the other remaining planets begin to spiral outward and settle into new and more distant orbits. Although Mercury is consumed in the Sun's red-giant inferno, Venus, like Earth, may escape being vaporized by also spiraling out to a more distant and safer orbit.

While hydrogen is burning in the shell around the helium core, the core continues to collapse and so heats up, since the hydrogen fusions are producing their energy outside the core. Eventually, the core temperature reaches 100,000,000 degrees. At this point the core helium—"ash" from the original core fusions—becomes fuel for a new set of reactions. This allows the core to stabilize once more and stop collapsing. In turn, the upward force of pressure on the outer layers of the star decreases, which allows the star to contract from its red giant size. For a hundred million years more, the Sun will shine more or less steadily as it burns its helium fuel.

Some 12.3 billion years from now, the Sun exhausts its helium fuel and then has a core of mostly carbon. Since the dying Sun cannot push the core temperature and pressure high enough to fuse carbon, gravity once again takes command, and the star collapses in on itself, as before. Once again the Sun's outer gas layers expand, and the Sun enters its second stage of red gianthood. This time its outer gases reach all the way out to Earth's present orbit. But by now Earth has long been gone in an orbit 1.7 times its former 93 million miles (150 million kilometers).

Over the next few million years another quarter of the Sun's mass will be lost to space as a *planetary nebula*, and its gravitational pull on its remaining planets has further weakened. All that will be left of the elderly Sun will be an exposed and collapsed core shrunken down to about the size of Earth. Shining only by heat left over from earlier times, the Sun will have become a star that astronomers call a *white dwarf*. With gravity the final victor in the game of tug-of-war, the Sun will shine on as an intensely bright but tiny object for a few billion more years. But with no new energy source, it can only grow dimmer and dimmer over that long period, eventually fading to an object best described as a *black dwarf*.

With the Sun's second shedding of mass and weakened gravitational pull, once again distant Earth and its siblings will spiral still farther away from their burned-out parent star. However, the black-dwarf relic of the Sun will still have enough mass to keep its children in tow. And one of those children will be Earth, by then a dead, shrunken, and frozen world, for its own internal fires will have cooled long ago.

With a retinue of perhaps seven planetary hulks, the black-dwarf Sun will continue its journey through the darkness of galactic space, circling the hub of the Milky Way and accompanied by countless other dead stars like it. By that time the galaxy itself will be dying. Although some star formation will continue to take place here and there, for the most part the galaxy will be a dark place, lighted so faintly that it will be invisible to its neighbors. However, since the rule seems to be that planets often form right along with a new star, some of the dying galaxy's new planets are likely to be spawning strange and marvelous life-forms of their own.

Before this inevitable scenario plays out, latter-day human species may see the end coming. Before it is too late, perhaps they will undertake the enormous task of abandoning dying Earth and colonizing a habitable planet belonging to a young and nearby Sunlike star.

Such notions may seem remote and farfetched to us today. And so they are, simply because there is so very much time left for the Sun to continue to nourish Earth and its marvelously diverse inhabitants. As William Fyfe reminds us, "Surely the knowledge of our past history must be considered when we plan the sustainable development for our future. This past record is preserved—in rocks, ice, tree-rings—and provides us with the 'archives' of our planet's history."

All we have to do is learn from those archives.

Glossary

abyssal plain A broad, flat region of the deep-ocean floor.

asteroid Any of millions of rock-metal fragments that range in size from that of a golf ball to that of a mountain, and that travel about the Sun in orbits between Mars and Jupiter.

asthenosphere A zone within the upper mantle where the rock is plastic and permits movement of the crust; it begins below a depth of about 60 miles (100 kilometers) and extends as deep as 450 miles (700 kilometers).

atomic clock The natural decay, at known rates, of certain radioactive elements such as uranium, potassium, and carbon into other elements. For instance, half the amount of uranium-238 in a sample decays into lead-206 in 4,510 million years; half the amount of carbon-14 in a sample decays into nitrogen-14 in 5,600 years.

Benioff Zone The zone of seismic activity that slopes downward from a trench on the ocean floor into the asthenosphere below. Named after Hugo Benioff, an American seismologist.

Big Bang The theory that the Universe was created some 12 or more billion years ago when a cosmic superatom, which contained all the matter and energy the Universe would ever have, exploded.

black dwarf A star that has passed through the white-dwarf stage and is radiating so little energy that it can no longer be observed directly.

body wave P-waves and S-waves, which travel through Earth when an earthquake occurs.

circumference The outer boundary, especially of a circle or sphere.

cleavage That property of a mineral that causes it to break apart along more or less smooth parallel planes.

continental drift The idea that the present continents once existed as a single supercontinent, and the supercontinent then broke into smaller continents that then "drifted" to their present positions.

continental rise A broad and gently sloping platform that may extend seaward from a continental slope.

continental slope The sloping seaward edge of a continental shelf.

convection cell Within Earth's mantle, one of a pair of convection currents of rock in a puttylike condition that transports heat and magma up into the crust.

core The innermost region of Earth. There is a solid inner core and a liquid outer core, and it is surrounded by the mantle.

Coriolis Effect An apparent force, caused by Earth's rotation, that tends to deflect winds and ocean currents. In the Northern Hemisphere the deflection is to the right of the path of motion, and in the Southern Hemisphere it is to the left. It is maximum at the poles and zero at the Equator. Named after Gaspard Coriolis, who first described the effect.

crust The outermost zone of Earth's surface. The continental crust is some 21 miles (35 kilometers) thick and is made of granite. The oceanic floor crust is some 3 miles (5 kilometers) thick and is made of basalt.

crystal A geometrically shaped solid that occurs naturally and exhibits smooth and shiny surfaces that represent an orderly arrangement of atoms.

crystalline structure The rigid and orderly pattern of atoms within a mineral.

cyanobacteria Bacteria that thrive in bright sunlight and make their own food out of free hydrogen and carbon dioxide in the atmosphere.

diameter The straight line passing through the center of a circle or a sphere and extending to the edges.

doldrums The belt of variable light or calm winds that occur at the Equator.

dynamo A rotating machine that changes an input of mechanical energy into an output of electrical energy; a dynamo can also do the reverse—convert an input of electrical energy into an output of mechanical energy.

element A substance that is made up entirely of the same kind of atoms and cannot be broken down into a simpler substance by chemical means. Examples are gold, oxygen, and lead.

fetch The length across which the wind blows in generating ocean waves.

fusion The union of atomic nuclei and, as a result, the building of the nuclei of more massive atoms. Hydrogen nuclei in the core of the Sun fuse and build up the nuclei of helium atoms.

galaxy A vast collection of stars, gas, and dust held together gravitationally. Spiral galaxies, the brightest of all galaxies, have a dense nucleus with less dense spiral arms. Our galaxy, the Milky Way, is a spiral galaxy containing a few hundred billion stars.

geologic column An idealized continuous column of rock that contains a complete geologic history, with the oldest rock layers at the bottom and the youngest layers at the top.

geosyncline A long trench that develops in Earth's crust and collects enormous amounts of sediments. The sediments may later become compressed into rock and thrust up as folded mountains.

Gondwana A continent formed during Earth's earlier history, when a large super-continent broke into a northern half called Laurasia and a southern half, which was Gondwana.

greenhouse effect The heat-trapping action of the atmosphere due to the blocking of long-wave radiation reflected from Earth's surface.

greenhouse gases Gases that contribute to the greenhouse effect and that include carbon dioxide, chlorofluorocarbons, nitrous oxide, methane, and water vapor.

Guyot A flat-topped seamount.

horse latitudes The high-pressure belt of air forming at about 30 degrees north and south latitudes with calm or gentle winds.

hot spot A region of melted rock within the mantle near the bottom of the lithosphere, with a diameter of a few hundred miles or kilometers. Hot spots seem to remain active for tens of millions of years.

hydrothermal vent A fracture in the seafloor that permits cool ocean water to enter and become heated by the hot rock below. The water then boils back up and spills out onto the ocean bottom. Water issuing from a hydrothermal vent is rich in dissolved minerals and is termed a "smoker."

igneous rock Rock formed when molten material flows up from deeper parts of Earth's crust and solidifies either within the crust or at the surface.

jet stream A high-altitude, fast-moving stream of westerly-flowing air. The stream is at an altitude of 10 to 15 miles (16 to 25 kilometers) and flows along at a speed of about 250 miles (402 kilometers) an hour.

Laurasia A continent formed during Earth's very early history when a large super-continent broke into a southern half and a northern half, the latter of which was Laurasia.

lava Volcanic outpourings of magma that cools and hardens to rock.

lithosphere Earth's rigid outer rock layer that occurs above the asthenosphere and includes the crust.

Lunar Day The 24-hour-and-50-minute period it takes for the Moon to return above a given point on Earth's surface.

magma Fluid rock material originating in the deeper parts of Earth's lithosphere. It is capable of forcing its way up through solid rock, and when flowing out over the surface, it is then called lava.

mantle That region of Earth's interior that lies between the outer boundary of the core and the lower boundary of the crust.

mesosphere The layer of atmosphere immediately above the stratosphere and below the thermosphere.

metamorphic rock Any rock mass of Earth's crust that has been changed in composition or texture through the action of heat, pressure, or chemically active fluids without involving the liquid phase.

meteoroid Any one of various rock and/or metal fragments orbiting the Sun singly or in swarms. Meteoroids often burn down through Earth's atmosphere as meteors and sometimes strike the ground as meteorites.

mineral Any element or compound found naturally in Earth, formed by a non-living process, having a fairly uniform chemical makeup and a rather constant set of physical properties, and having a fixed and orderly internal arrangement of its atoms.

Moho The boundary between Earth's crust and mantle, where there is a sharp increase in the velocity of seismic waves, named in honor of Andrija Mohorovičić.

neap tide Weak tides raised when the Moon is at first and third quarters with the Sun and Moon forming a right angle.

ozone layer A layer of a gas, composed of three atoms of oxygen (O^3) as opposed to the oxygen we breathe (O^2), in the upper atmosphere that protects living organisms by filtering out a substantial amount of ultraviolet radiation from the Sun.

P-wave A seismic body wave capable of traveling through solids and liquids alike by the alternate compression and expansion of the solid or liquid it is passing through.

Pangaea The single supercontinent that existed about 220 million years ago. By about 135 million years ago, Pangaea had broken up and drifted apart into two pieces.

planet A celestial object that shines by reflected light from a star around which the planet is held gravitationally captive and revolves. There are nine known primary planets in the Solar System.

planetary nebula A nebula, such as the Ring Nebula in Lyra, once mistakenly thought to be a planet. The faint greenish color of a planetary nebula gives it the appearance of the planet Uranus. Such a nebula actually is a gigantic cloud of gas exploded off a star and enclosing the star within a diffuse sphere of gases.

planetesimals Clumps of solid matter that formed out of the solar disk material in the early years of the Solar System's formation. The planetesimals were made up of rock, or rock mixed with iron and other metals, and ices.

plate (See plate tectonics.)

plate tectonics The widely accepted notion that there are six major "plates" and about a dozen smaller ones that form Earth's lithosphere. The continents, along with sections of the ocean floor, are pushed about like giant rafts of rock due to the movement of the puttylike rock of the asthenosphere below.

plume An upward flow of molten rock from the lower mantle to the crust, believed to form hot spots.

polar easterlies Belts of winds occurring at extreme latitudes in both hemispheres. They blow out of the northeast in the Northern Hemisphere and out of the southeast in the Southern Hemisphere.

precession Earth's circular wobbling on its axis, which makes one complete circle every 25,800 years.

prevailing westerlies The winds that blow out of the west from about 30 degrees to 60 degrees north and south latitudes. Those in the Northern Hemisphere blow out of the southwest, and those in the Southern Hemisphere blow out of the northwest.

radioactive heating The natural heating of Earth's rock material due to the spontaneous decay of radioactive elements, such as uranium and potassium.

radius One half the diameter.

red giant An enormous star that shines with a reddish light because of its relatively low surface temperature (about 3,000 kelvins). It is now thought that most stars go through a red-giant stage after they exhaust their core hydrogen fuel.

rift valley A fracture in Earth's crust along which molten rock from the mantle wells up and flows out onto the surrounding land (or seafloor). A region of East Africa and the Middle East.

rock A solid, naturally occurring mixture of minerals. Rocks often contain a mixture of minerals, particles of other rocks, and the remains of once-living matter.

rock cycle The sequence of changes Earth materials pass through when influenced by geologic processes.

S-wave Seismic body wave that travels by side-to-side or up-and-down motion along the path of the wave train. S-waves travel through solids but not liquids.

seafloor spreading The widening of the ocean floor due to the upwelling of magma through ocean ridges, or fracture lines, that extend for hundreds of miles along the ocean floor. The Midatlantic Ridge is one such fracture line.

seamounts Undersea, steep-sided volcanic peaks; also called guyots.

sedimentary rock Rock formed from clay, lime, sand, gravel, and sometimes plant and/or animal remains. The materials have been compacted and hardened under great weight and pressure for long periods of time.

sediments Loose bits and pieces of clay, mud, sand, gravel, lime, and other Earth materials that are washed into the oceans, lakes, and rivers.

solar day The length of time it takes Earth to rotate once on its axis, using the departure and return of the Sun to a given meridian; measured from noon to noon or midnight to midnight.

solar wind Streams of charged particles (protons and electrons) that are blown off by the Sun and sweep through the Solar System.

spring tide The high tide raised when the Sun, Earth, and Moon are aligned either at full moon or new moon, at which times the gravitational force of the Sun and Moon reinforce each another.

star A hot, glowing sphere of gas that emits energy by nuclear fusions. The Sun is a typical, and our closest, star.

stratosphere The layer of atmosphere that lies above the troposphere and below the mesosphere. The stratosphere is Earth's second air layer and extends from a height of about 7 miles (12 kilometers) to about 30 miles (48 kilometers).

subduction zone The region along which one plate collides with and descends beneath a neighboring plate. Part of the depressed plate's edge then melts.

supernova A giant and massive star that has exhausted its fuel for fusion reactions and explodes, casting off a large part of its mass. Supernovas may be observed over a week or more as especially brilliant objects.

surface wave Seismic waves that travel along the surface of Earth's crust. Surface waves cause all the damage during an earthquake.

terrestrial planets The inner planets of the Solar System—Mercury, Venus, Earth, and Mars.

thermosphere The top layer of Earth's atmosphere, which begins at a height of about 50 miles (80 kilometers) and blends with outer space.

tidal bore A sudden rush of water from an incoming tide that surges forcefully and rapidly up a river when the shape of the river's mouth is configured in a certain way.

trade winds The two wind belts that extend from the margin of the doldrums to about 30 degrees north and south latitude. In the Northern Hemisphere they blow out of the northeast, and in the Southern Hemisphere out of the southeast.

troposphere The layer of atmosphere that extends from the ground to a height of about 7 miles (12 kilometers), where most of our weather occurs.

tsunami A gigantic, destructive ocean wave triggered by an earthquake in the seafloor.

turbidity current A powerful mudslide down a continental slope. Sediment may cascade down a slope at speeds up to 50 miles (80 kilometers) an hour.

ultraviolet radiation Short-wave radiation from the Sun—the harmful radiation that causes sunburn and skin cancer. Most of the radiation is absorbed by the ozone layer in the upper atmosphere.

wave crest The top edge of a wave.

wave period The length of time between crests as a train of waves passes a fixed point.

wave trough The bottom point between two successive wave crests.

white dwarf A very small star that radiates stored energy rather than new energy generated through nuclear fusions. The Sun is destined to become a white dwarf after it goes through the red-giant stage.

zodiacal light A faint band of light that extends along the ecliptic (the Sun's apparent path across the sky). It is light reflected by dust particles and is best seen on clear nights in March and September.

Further Reading

Brown, Lester, R., Christopher Flavin, and Hal Kane. *Vital Signs: 1996.* World-watch Institute, W.W. Norton & Company, 1996.

——— et al. *State of the World.* Worldwatch Institute, W.W. Norton & Company, 1997.

Clark, William C. "Managing Planet Earth." *Scientific American*, September 1989.

Clayton, Keith. *Crust of the Earth.* The Natural History Press, 1967.

Cowen, Ron. "The Once and Future Sun." *Science News*, pp. 204–205, March 26, 1994.

———. "Meteorite Still Holds Inklings of Life." *Science News*, p. 190, March 29, 1997.

———. "C'est la Vie." *Science News*, pp. 284–285, November 1, 1997.

Dathe, David. Earth: *The Science of Our Planet.* Earth Science Reader, Wm. C. Brown Publishers, 1994.

Dopyera, Caroline. "The Iron Hypothesis." *Earth,* pp. 26–33, October 1996.

Dorr, Ann. *Minerals—Foundations of Society.* American Geological Institute, 1987.

Earth Magazine, December 1996. A special issue about many aspects of planet Earth.

Flanagan, Ruth. "Engineering a Cooler Planet." *Earth,* pp. 34–39, October 1996.

———, and Tom Yulsman. "On Thin Ice." *Earth,* pp. 44–51, April 1996.

Fredrickson, James K., and Tullis C. Onstott. "Microbes Deep Inside the Earth." *Scientific American*, pp. 68–73, October 1996.

Gallant, Roy A. *Our Universe.* National Geographic Society, 1994.

———. *A Young Person's Guide to Science.* Macmillan, 1993.

———. *The Peopling of Planet Earth.* Macmillan, 1990.

———. *Before the Sun Dies: The Story of Evolution.* Macmillan, 1989.

———. *The Ice Ages.* Watts, 1985.

———. *Geysers.* Watts, 1997.

———. *Limestone Caves.* Watts, 1997.

———, and Christopher J. Schuberth. *Discovering Rocks and Minerals.* The Natural History Press, 1967.

Gaskell, T.H. *World Beneath the Oceans.* The Natural History Press, 1964.

Gibson, Everett K., Jr., David S. McKay, Kathie Thomas–Keptra, and Christopher S. Romanek. "The Case of Relic Life on Mars." *Scientific American*, pp. 58–665, December 1997. Natural History Press, 1964.

Hamblin, W .K., and Laura Hamblin. "Fire and Water: the Making of the Grand Canyon." *Natural History*, pp. 34–41, September 1997.

Hansen, Gunnar. *Islands at the Edge of Time: A Journey to America's Barrier Islands.* Island Press, 1993.

Hart, Stephen. "Tubeworm Travels." *Earth,* pp. 48–53, June 1997.

Kargel, Jeffrey S., and Robert G. Strom. "Global Climatic Change on Mars." *Scientific American,* pp. 80–88, November 1996.

Lang, Kenneth R. "SOHO Reveals the Secrets of the Sun." *Scientific American*, pp. 40–47, March 1997.

Linden, Eugene. "Antarctica: Warnings from the Ice." *Time*, pp. 54–59, April 14, 1997.

Lutz, Richard A. "Rebirth of a Deep-Sea Vent." *National Geographic*, pp. 114–126, November 1994.

Mestel, Rosie. "Mush in the Mantle." *Earth*, pp. 22–25, February 1997.

Mills, Cynthia. "Big Water." *Earth*, pp. 62–63, October 1996.

Monastersky, R. "Continents Grew Early in Earth's History." *Science News*, p. 70, February 1, 1997.

———."Deep Dwellers." *Science News*, pp. 192–193, March 29, 1997.

———. "Global Graveyard." *Science News*, pp. 46–47, July 19, 1997.

———. "Spying on El Niño." *Science News*, pp. 268–270, October 25, 1997.

————. "The West Coast's Roving Real Estate." *Science News*, p. 164, September 13, 1997.

Mungall, Constance, and Digby J. McLaren. *Planet Under Stress*. Oxford University Press, 1996.

Parker, Samantha. "Mars Global Surveyor." *Sky and Telescope*, pp. 32–34, January 1998.

Parks, Noreen. "Loihi Rumbles to Life." *Earth*, pp. 442–449, April 1997.

Pendick, Daniel. "Himalayan High Tension." *Earth*, pp. 46–53, October 1996.

————. "The Dust Ages." *Earth*, pp. 22–23, 66–67, June 1996.

Pendleton, Yvonne J., and Jack D. Farmer. "Life: A Cosmic Imperative?" *Sky & Telescope*, pp. 42–47, July 1997.

Penvenne, Laura Jean. "Blame It on the Sun." *Earth*, pp. 22–23, August 1996.

Peterson, Carol Collins. "Welcome to Mars." *Sky and Telescope*, pp. 34–39, October 1997.

Pielou, E.C. *After the Ice Age*. University of Chicago Press, 1991.

Pinter, Nicholas, and Mark T. Brandon. "How Erosion Builds Mountains." *Scientific American*, pp. 74–79, April 1997.

Pratson, Lincoln F., and William F. Haxby. "Panoramas of the Seafloor." *Scientific American*, pp. 82–87, June 1997.

Rona, Peter A. "Deep-Sea Geysers of the Atlantic." *National Geographic*, pp. 105–109, October 1992.

Sampson, Russell D. "Jewels of the Sky." *Earth*, pp. 54–59, October 1996.

Schmidt, Karen. "Life on the Brink." *Earth*, pp. 26–33, April 1997.

Schneider, David. "The Rising Seas." *Scientific American*, pp. 112–117, March 1997.

————. "Hot-Spotting." *Scientific American*, pp. 22–24, August 1997.

Schneider, Stephen H. *Global Warming*. Sierra Club Books, 1989.

Scovil, Jeff. "Crystal Clear." *Earth*, pp. 58–59, April 1997.

Stevens, Jane Ellen. "Exploring Antarctic Ice." *National Geographic*, pp. 36–53, May 1996.

Taylor, S. Ross, and Scott M. McLennan. "The Evolution of Continental Crust." *Scientific American*, pp. 76–81, January 1996.

Tibbetts, John. "Plagued by Climate." *Earth,* pp. 20–21, 76–77, April 1996.

Vogel, Shawna. "Living Planet." *Earth,* pp. 27–35, April 1996.

———. "Has Global Warming Begun?" *Earth*, pp. 24–34, December 1995.

Wickelbren, Ingrid. "Matching Tops and Bottoms." *Earth*, pp. 22–24, June 1997.

World Watch Publication, "Playing God with Climate." Vol. 10, No. 6, December 1997, World Watch Institute, Washington, D. C.

Yulsman, Tom. "The Seafloor Laid Bare." *Earth*, pp. 42–51, June 1996.

Planet Earth Online—Web Sites

The Aurora Page:
http://www.geo.mtu.edu/weather/aurora/

Earth Online:
http://ritter.wadsworth.com

Earth Science:
http://www.ciesin.org/

The Earth System Science Community:
http://www.circles.org

Global Warming Update:
http://www.ncdc.noaa.gov/gblwrmupd/global.html

Hubble Space Telescope:
http://www.stsci.edu/Latest.html

Jet Propulsion Laboratory:
http://www.jpl.nasa.gov/archive/images. html

Johnson Space Center:
http://images. jsc.nasa.gov/

JPL Physical Oceanography Archive:
http://seazar.jpl.nasa/gov

Marine Geology, National Marine and Coastal Geology Program:
http://walrus.wr.usgs.gov

The Museum of Paleontology:
http://ucmp1.berkeley.edu/

NASA *Hot Topics*:
http://www.nasa.gov.nasa/nasa_hottopics.html

NASA Today:
http://www.hq.nasa.gov/office/pao/newsroom/today.html

National Earthquake Information Center:
htpp://neic.cr.usgs.gov/

National Geophysical Data Center:
http://www.ngdc.noaa.gov/

National Museum of Natural History (Smithsonian):
http://nmnhgoph.si.edu/

Ocean Planet: Smithsonian Institution
http://seawifs.gsfc.nasa.gov/ocean_planet.html

Ozone Action Page:
http://www.ozone.org

Rosenstiel School of Marine and Atmospheric Science Home Page:
http://www.rsmas.miami.edu/

Royal Tyrrell Museum:
http://tyrrell.magtech.ab.ca/

Space Science and Engineering Center (SSEC):
http://www.ssec.wisc.edu/vw.html

Sunrise/Sunset/Twilight and Moonrise/Moonset/Phase:
http://tycho.usno.navy.mil/srss.html

University of Illinois—The Daily Planet:
http://www.atmos.uiuc.edu

U.S. Cities Weather and Forecasts:
http://www.mit.edu:8001/weather/usa.html

U.S. Geological Survey:
http://www.usgs.gov/

USGS Earth and Environmental Science Index:
http://www.usgs.gov/network/science/earth/earth.html

USGS Hawaii Volcano Watch Reports:
http://www.soest.hawaii.edu/hvo/

USGS Internet Resources on Earthquakes:
http://www.usgs.gov/network/science/earth/earthquake.html

USGS Minerals Page:
http://minerals.er.usgs.gov

Virtually Hawaii:
http://www.satlab.hawaii.edu/space/hawaii/

Volcano Information Center:
http://magic.geol.ucsb.edu/~fisher

Volcano World:
http://volcano.und.nodak.edu/

What's Erupting Now:
http://volcano.und.nodak.edu/vwdocs/current_volcs/current.html

Woods Hole, USGS Atlantic Marine Geology:
http://woodshole.er.usgs.gov/

Magazines:

Earth:
http://www.kalmbach.com/earth/earthmag.html

Meteorite!:
http://www.meteor.co.nz

National Geographic:
http://www.nationalgeographic.com

Scientific American:
http://www.sciam.com/

Sky & Telescope:
http://www.skypub.com/

Index

Page numbers for illustrations are in boldface.

crystalline structure,
33–36, **34**, **35**
currents, ocean, 86–89,
88, 98–99, **99**
cyanide, 21
cyanobacteria, 22
Cygnus the Swan, 14

Darwin, Charles, 106–107
day, length of, 91, 92–94,
93
Deccan Plateau, 108
deep-ocean basin,
104–105
deep-sea fan, 98
Devonian period, 27
diameter, Earth's, 43, 75
diamonds, 31, 36, 104
doldrums, 71, **73**
dynamos, 54

Earth
age of, 20–21
axis of, 52–53, 55, 75
climate, 66, 75–78
core of, 22, **44**, 48–55
crust of, 23, 30–44, 57
and day length, 91,
92–94, **93**
early youth of, 21–22
future of, 65–66, 78,
93, 110, 131–41
heavenly bodies striking,
17–18, **18**, **19**, 22
landform development,
25–29, **26**
later youth of, 23–25
magnetism of, 50–55,
51, **52**
mantle of, **44**, 44–48,
55–57, **56**
measuring, 43–45, **46**
pressure of, 57–58
temperature of, 58
earthquakes. *See also* plate
tectonics

and deep-ocean trenches,
100–101, **101**
depth of, 56
frequency, 46
shock waves from,
47–48
and tsunamis, 85
and turbidity currents,
98
East Pacific Rise, 62, 102
echo sounder, 95–96
elements
compound, 31
heavy, 15
native, 31
radioactive, 41
Elsasser, Walter M., 54, 55
Emperor Seamount chain,
109
energy
nuclear, 16
from start of universe,
11
from Sun, 16, 22, 69,
137–39
Environmental Protection
Agency, 135
EPA (Environmental
Protection Agency),
135
Equatorial belt, 70–71, **73**
Equatorial Countercurrent,
88
Eratosthenes, 43–44, 45
evolution, biological, 66
extinction, biological, 66

fan, deep-sea, 98
Faraday, Michael, 54
fault line, 63–64
feldspar, 32
fertilizers, 136
fetch, 82
flood basalts, 108
formaldehyde, 21
fossil magnetic fields, 126

fossils, 36
and Antarctica, 65
and climate change,
75–76
in coal and rock, 36
of marine organisms,
92
in sedentary rock strata,
40, 41
fracture zones, 102
Franklin, Benjamin, **88**
Freon, 134–35
fusion reactions, 15, 137
Fyfe, William S., 131, 141

Galapagos Mid-Ocean
Ridge, 103
galaxies, formation of, **12**,
12–15, **13**
gemstones, 32–33
geological periods, 25–29,
40–42
geologic column, 40–42
geosynclines, 25–26
geysers, undersea, 103,
129
Gilbert, William, 52–53
glacial cycles, 76–78, **77**,
78
glaciers, 29, **77**
global warming, **68**,
132–36
gold, 21, 31, 81, 104
Gondwana, 25
granite, 21, 24, 36, 57,
126
graphite, 31, 36
gravity
and Earth's atmos-
phere, 67
and Earth's axis, 75
effect on Sun, 138
of Mars, 119
and planet formation,
16
and star formation, 13

and tides, 24, **90**, 90–94, **93**
and tsunamis, 85
greenhouse effect, 117–19, **118**, 131–33
Greenland ice cap, **78**
Gulf of California, 62
Gulf Stream, 87–88, **88**
Gutenberg, Beno, 48
guyots, 105, 109

Hale-Bopp comet, 18
Hawaiian Islands, 107–110
heavy elements, 15
helium
    at birth of universe, 11
    in formation of stars, 13–15
    in planets, 16–17, 21
    in solar energy, 137–40
Hercules, **12**, **13**
Hess, Harry H., 105
Himalayan Mountains, 28
Holocene period, 41
Hooper, Peter, 108
hornblende, 32
horse latitudes, 71, **73**
hot spots, 65, 107–108
Hubble Space Telescope, 12
Human beings composed of atoms, 19
Humboldt Current, 89
hydrocarbons, 129–30. *See also* oil
hydrogen
    in birth of universe, 11
    in formation of stars, 13–15
    in planets, 16–17, 21
    and solar energy, 137–39
hydrogen chloride, 116
hydrogen fluoride, 116
hydrothermal vents, 102–103

ice ages, 27, 29, 76–78, **77**, **78**
icefalls, **77**
Iceland, 23, 62, **63**, 108
igneous rock, 36, **37**, **38**
impact craters, 16–18, **18**
India, 28
iron, 21, 50, 54–55, 103

Jeffreys, Harold, 50
jet stream, 72
Jordan Valley, 22–23
Jupiter, 113, **113**
Jurassic period, 28

kaolin, 32, 36
Kasting, James F., 138
Kilauea, 109
Kuiper Belt, 18

Labrador Current, 88–89
Laue, Max von, 35
Laurasia, 25
lava, 36, **38**, **52**, 102, 116
lead, 32, 41, 103
Lehmann, I., 50
life
    on Mars, 127–30
    in seas, 89, 95, 103, 129, 135
lime, 39
limestone, 39
lithosphere, **56**, 57, 102
Loihi Seamount, 109–110
lunar day, 91

magma, 23, 36, **38**, 102. *See also* hot spots
magnesium, 81
magnetism, 50–55, **51**, **52**, 126
magnetite, 32
manganese, 104
mantle, **44**, 44–48, 55–57, **56**

margins, continental, 96–101
Marianas Trench, 100
Mars, 119–30, **120**, **122**
Mauna Loa, 109
Mediterranean Sea, 66
Mendocino Fracture Zone, 102
Mercury, **112**, 112–13
mesosphere, 69
Mesozoic period, 41–42, 76
metamorphic rock, **37**, **38**, 39
meteoroids, 16–17, 18–19, 22
methane, 16–17, 21, 22
mica, 32, 35, **35**
Midatlantic Ridge, 61–62, **63**
mid-ocean ridges, 23–24, 61–62, **63**, 101–105
Milky Way, 13–19
minerals, 30–36, 42, 103–104. *See also* rocks; specific minerals
Moho, 48
Mohorovičić, Andrija, 48, 57
Moon
    creation of, 24–25
    "escape" from Earth, 92–93, **93**
    and tides, **90**, 90–94, **93**
mountains. *See also* volcanoes; specific mountains
continental, 102
undersea, 23–24, 61–62, **63**, 101–105
Mount Russel icefall, 77

native elements, 31